Trying to SEE

An Eclectic Devotional

By
Jeff Hill

Keep looking
JHill
Romans 8:31

To Chris
for your encouragement to keep writing,
honest feedback, and time.

Author's Note

For those of us who have abandoned the myth that matter is eternal and the illusion that reason alone answers life's big questions, all that is left is God. It follows that we find within us a deeply rooted impulse to encounter Him, or at the least, interpret Him. This impulse does not easily subside. On one hand we aren't actually going to see Him. He chooses invisibility. If He were to visually reveal Himself it might not be good for us; at least that's what He told Moses. Still we do pursue and our pursuit is problematic. Can God really be known? Surely we realize He is vastly infinite. By nature He is beyond our understanding. C.S. Lewis referred to Him the great "Other." If we did have Him orderly arranged in our meager intellect, He would no longer be God. Yet here we are. We have scriptural admonition to "seek Him with all our heart" and a clearly prescribed boundary that the best we can hope for is to "see in a mirror dimly." Such is the realm of our odyssey.

I think most of us have caught our glimpses, obscure as they may be, during some of the little times in our lives. Not many of us have taken our sandals off at a burning bush or stood in the opening of a cave receiving instructions from a voice in the clouds. Rather, through the Word, or music, or prayer, or most likely while simply experiencing life, we've had a "God moment," maybe more than one. If we have, we need to embrace those interludes as a gift. Best we receive them humbly, hold them close, and ponder them thoroughly.

This book is a simple collection of my thoughts and experiences as I've muddled my way through life's attempts at seeing Him, seeing where I fit in His world, and watched as others have struggled to do the same. Sometimes the struggle results in moments of beauty and grace. Other times, not so much. There is gold, precious stones, and solid wood in all our lives. There is also hay, chaff, and stubble.

The meditations and prayers are my own and the vignettes are based on true events I have personally experienced, personally observed, or they stem from interviews with the actual people involved. Names and locations have been changed for confidentiality. In a couple of the stories I have combined two people into one character. At times I've used first person as a literary device. Hence, the "I" may not always be me.

If one episode, one commentary, or one prayer, lifts one person to a place with a better view, that would be a good thing.

J. Hill

Contents

243897

On a summer day when the sun is on high beam and the breezes are welcome caresses, Lake Superior is a visual and sensory force. The water is so rare a blue that a proper adjective cannot be found to describe it. If you are standing along Duluth's high ridge you can see the sweeping curve of the earth and watch the thousand-foot ore carriers fall off the edge. From Park Point looking back toward the city, black hulled, high mast sailboats skim the surface and large cruisers manned by happy faces come and go at the marina. You'd swear you were looking at a village planted on a steep hillside along the Mediterranean. Wading in forty-degree water however, quickly cools off that illusion. If you're in a boat a few miles off shore, a penetrating, primordial awareness overwhelms a person. It is an awareness of the unbelievable enormity of the earth and its largest fresh water ocean.

When my children were still living at home we'd try to get up there as many summers as we could. Duluth meant fun places to eat and hanging out at the lift bridge. There, we could watch giant ships from all over the world squeeze through the narrow canal, their rotating radar scanners barely slipping under the raised deck of the iconic bridge. Many of the crew would be out on deck waving a happy hello to the crowds pressing on the rail.

We also enjoyed the train ride. The city runs an open-air train made of passenger cars with no walls or windows. You sit on simple wood benches situated perpendicular to the sides of the car so you can face each other and still look out in both directions. The train creeps its way from the waterfront up to the high ridge of the city and on through to the northeastern outskirts of town.

On one such excursion two elderly ladies sat down across from the four of us. They were both short and slight. They moved slowly but were not frail. They boarded arm and arm and remained that way while seated. Their silver hair was professionally done and their make-up was just so. They wore stylish clothing and each one was adorned with earrings, bracelets, and wedding rings with diamonds that were not bought at the mall. One couldn't help but assume they were sisters.

As the train crawled along, they started commenting to one another about what they were seeing. Occasionally, they would slip into an unfamiliar language and almost whisper to each other. Their enjoyment of the vistas of the crystal blue sea was obvious.

After ten minutes or so, one of the ladies turned her attention to us and asked, "Are you locals?"

"Yes we are."

"We've heard about a place called Palisades Head and wondered if it was worth the trip further up the north shore?"

"It is spectacular and worth the drive." I assured them.

Their query opened the door for some informal introductions. Their names were Hattie and Lillian. An easy comfortableness settled in on the six of us, and we carried on with a light friendly conversation.

For the first time since we met them they unclasped their arms and created a slight space between themselves on the bench. Hattie's sleeves were three quarters length. As she and Lillian adjusted their seating and unlocked arms her inner forearm became visible exposing something that looked like a tattoo scar. It was old and small.

Hattie noticed that we noticed. She wasn't offended. She actually leaned forward, held out her arm and gave us a closer look. It was a number: 243897.

It happened that at this time, my daughter was going through a period in her early middle school education where she was studying all things Nazi, Jewish, and WWII. She had read Ann Frank, Number the Stars, and anything about Corrie ten Boom. She knew before the rest of us what the numbers on Hattie's arm meant. She immediately crossed the aisle and sat next to her. Hattie gently clasped my daughter's hand and gave her a little squeeze and allowed her to slowly graze her index finger over the numbers. She then wrapped her arm around my daughter's so now they were ones who were arm and arm.

"We were about your age." Hattie said, breaking the silence. "We met at Majdanek."

She motioned to Lillian. Lillian slid up her sleeve just enough to reveal her scar also. The numbers were not as clear as Hattie's, but there was no mistaking them for anything else.

The ladies went on to tell a heart-wrenching story of terror, brutality, loss...and survival.

"Majdanek started out as a factory camp and eventually morphed into an extermination camp," she explained. "It was a place where nostril violating stench and chimneys blackened by unholy fires provided unrelenting daily torment. By some miracle we both remained sane. We first noticed each other in a food line. Our mothers, fathers, brothers, and sisters were all gone. We became inseparable."

"That is why we survived." Lillian added.

Hattie continued.

"One night we heard gunfire and shouting, followed by big explosions in the distance. The Germans fled the camp. By morning the gates were unguarded, yet none of us left. We were emaciated and pale. We didn't have enough strength to walk anywhere anyway. We all stood silently at the edge of the fences, staring into the distance, waiting for we knew not what. The Allies came the next afternoon. We didn't know who they were, or why they were there. But we knew they weren't the Nazis."

Then Lillian recounted an unshakable memory.

"There was a tall man in a brown uniform. He broke off a piece of bread and held it out for me. When I reached through the fence to take it I looked up. I still remembered the officer's eyes, vividly. They were as exhausted as mine and he was crying."

Hattie knew of an uncle who had immigrated to America before the hostilities broke out in Europe. The uncle took both girls in and raised them as sisters until adulthood. They grew, married,

11

had families, and lived full lives. They never lost contact with each other. Now in their twilight years they were both widows. Hattie lived in California and Lillian in Manitoba. For the last twelve or so summers they would pick a city in the U.S. to vacation together. The city had to have a university and be close to natural wonders. Had to have a university because they would audit a class during their visit. As Hattie put it, "We need to keep learning new things to stay sharp." Natural wonders because, "Who wants to sit in a classroom all day?"

All too soon the train was pulling back into the station. My family's little ten-mile tourist ride had become much more than merely taking in the views. We'd been transported back in time to Eastern Europe with two young Jewish orphan girls.

My daughter and Hattie were still arm and arm. She told Hattie about the books she had been reading and a movie she'd seen.

"When I think about all that stuff I have trouble believing there is a God."

Hattie squeezed her arm a little tighter and leaned in. "There has to be a God my dear."

"Why?"

"Because we can still love."

"We love because He first loved us."
1 John 4:19

Irrevocable

If you drive through Bancroft you'll see a grain elevator and an abandoned filling station. That's all there is and all there ever was. If you drive slowly enough, however, you might notice a small, clapboard church about a quarter of a mile off the main road. Most of the paint has weathered off the outside walls. Walls that were kept impeccably white when its small congregation met there. The windows now are empty openings. The bell is still in the steeple although its gears have rusted and the pull rope is long gone. The wood floor still bears the marks of anchored pews and restless feet. An outline of a large cross on the front wall is less faded than the rest of the wall where it used to preside.

Hundreds of these timeworn churches dot the landscape of the Midwest. Although they're now deserted, they hold countless stories of baptisms, weddings, picnics, confirmations, Sunday school classes, funerals, candle light Christmas Eve services, Easter morning breakfasts, and conversations united by church basement coffee.

They also whisper stories of God, speaking and calling.

Sixty some years ago the little church in Bancroft still had a vibrant heartbeat. It was their annual tradition to hold vacation Bible school beginning the last Monday in July. Young children would come in from the surrounding farms and hear the great stories of Noah and the Ark, Moses and the burning bush, Joseph and Pharaoh, Daniel in the lion's den, and of course, Jesus. This particular summer was Billy Stedman's first chance to attend. He was five.

Leona Carver was the teacher assigned to the five and six year olds. Her auburn hair was hinting streaks of gray. She was thinner than most of the ladies in town and always wore a neatly fitted dress. She had a matter of fact way about her and took vacation Bible school seriously. She prayerfully prepared lessons and went out of

13

her way to have props and visual aids. On the last day she always gave an age appropriate account of Calvary, followed by a simple gospel invitation.

It is a testimony to the grace of God and the simplicity of the gospel that a five year old can comprehend His invitation. Young Billy Stedman understood that God's love was for him. While the other kids ran outside for kickball, he went back to see Mrs. Carver. In the basement of this two-room country church she let him know that he could give his life to God.

In his own childlike way, he did.

When he told his mom and brother what happened, he sensed they didn't fully understand. Even as a child he understood their reaction didn't match the magnitude of the event that had occurred within him.

Billy's childhood proceeded on in normal fashion: frogs, snakes, tree houses, bikes, and baseball.

Seven years later the church hosted a missionary. He spoke at a special Saturday night service.

Billy was there.

God called.

It wasn't an audible voice. It wasn't a face to face, Moses on the mountain exchange. Yet it was a clear, unmistakable, message. "You are going to be a missionary."

When the visiting missionary offered to meet and pray with anyone who felt the call to missions, Billy was first in line. That night when he went to bed, thoughts of Africa kept him from falling asleep.

Yet, his life proceeded on in normal fashion: school, sports, work, cars, college, marriage, and a job.

The foreign missionary vision slowly faded.

When children came along, Billy's teacher's salary didn't adequately provide for his family. He took on a part time sales job. It was a good fit. He loved the art of the deal. Soon he was making more money in sales than he was teaching. He quit and started his own store. Before long he was buying retail spaces and renting to other businesses. This led to even larger real estate development projects, commercial as well as residential. Billy became a successful and established metropolitan businessman. He was a long way from Bancroft.

The call of God to become a foreign missionary had dimmed, but hadn't completely vanished. When he attended mission presentations, however, he always left a little hollow. All the foreign missionaries were language experts. They were Bible school or seminary trained, and they dragged their families with them to the field, willing or not. Billy's skills were "secular." He was about property acquisition and development, training and managing people, having a vision for a project, casting that vision and marshaling it to completion. He was also confident his family was not interested in moving to Africa. He finally concluded he wasn't mission field material. Reluctantly, he resigned himself to the idea that maybe financial backing was going to be his life long contribution to foreign missions.

God's idea was a bit bigger.

One day, just in passing when Billy heard that someone was coming to his local church to talk about outreaches to Russia, a bell went off. It was the old steeple bell in the white clapboard church ringing out that it was "time" to come inside. Billy made sure he was there.

The presenter was looking for people willing to do a short-term trip to help run a summer Bible camp. Five months later Billy was in the middle of the Ukraine.

The camp conditions were disturbing. The buildings had leaky roofs and broken doors. The dorms had rusty WWII era bunk frames with no mattresses. The bathrooms were foul with dysfunctional plumbing. The grounds were not mowed and the footpaths were overgrown with weeds. Prisons had better food and there was no health service. The kids who came to the camp however, were spiritually starving. They drank up every word of the gospel as fast as it was delivered and asked for more. This was not lost on Billy. He caught a vision for what a camp could be, what it

15

should not be, and a larger scope of what the youth in the Ukraine urgently needed.

God had one more thing to say. "Now I will show you why your life has gone the way it has."

What the Lord needed was a man who could see the potential in a piece of property, broker a deal to purchase it, organize the human and material resources to develop it, secure someone to staff it, and keep a flow of people coming who could improve and maintain it. God needed a man of compassion who grasped the human need and understood the power of the gospel.

Billy was His man. Bible school trained linguists need not apply.

Today there is a Bible camp, conference center, vocational school, and small business training center in southern Ukraine. It has an envied food service, beautiful grounds, and fully restored buildings. A former Soviet youth camp, it was purchased in a state of disrepair for a price substantially below market value. Volunteers from Billy's home church have taken a hundred plus short-term trips to paint, plumb, landscape, repair, rewire, reroof, and resupply the compound. A highly respected international outreach organization staffs and runs the center with locals, that they train. Money from a generous and ever expanding group of benefactors continues to fund the operation. Most importantly, the stories of individuals, home and abroad, whose lives have been forever changed, takes your breath away.

And Billy Stedman became a missionary to a foreign land.

"For the gifts and calling of God are irrevocable."

Romans 11:29

R & D Version

"Helen! Have you seen my red tie?"

"Did you try your tie rack?"

"Very funny."

"Wear a blue one."

"I am going to wear my red one."

"All right. But you better hurry up. We shouldn't be late."

Gerard found the red tie wrapped around a hanger with one of his other suits.

"Got it." He yelled.

The right clothes for the right occasion was important to Gerard Lansky. The dark blue suit with a crisply ironed and starched white shirt and red tie was his, "this is serious business" uniform.

"You seem a little riled up. Want me to drive?" she asked.

"I'll drive." It was not up for discussion.

The Lansky's driveway was over a half mile long. It ran past a horse pasture bordered by a white rail fence, then through a grove of majestic red oaks. Helen didn't say anything more until they were well down the road.

"I wish you'd calm down. I don't want to go in there if you're going to be angry."

"Don't tell me to calm down. I do some of my best work when I'm angry. I'll calm down after I'm done with this guy. Who does he think he's working for anyway?"

Helen had one more argument up her sleeve, but she decided to save it for later.

Supposedly the Lansky's were on their way to parent-teacher conferences at their son's school. However, one of those conferences was going to be an employee, employer conference. Gerard had determined that it would not go well for the employee.

Heritage Academy was situated in an upper middle class suburb.

17

It was a non-denominational Christian school with a student body that represented families from over 40 different churches. The school was only 12 years old but already had an excellent facility with room to grow, acreage to expand, and a rising academic reputation in the Christian community. Gerard Lansky was the chairman of the board of directors. His deep pockets helped hire legal advice for the articles of incorporation and helped to secure the original mortgage. In his mind, Heritage Academy was his school, and in many ways it was.

He had been an air force officer who had to retire prematurely because of a health condition. He had saved a nice sum in his twenty plus years of service. That money, combined with a keen business sense, hard work, and some timely real estate deals eventually allowed him to own a series of car dealerships, two strip malls, and a large parking ramp out by the airport. All of which, he controlled with a tight rein.

His penchant for holding a firm grip on his various enterprises held true for Heritage Academy also. It was his dream to have a Christian school of high quality academic, artistic, and athletic opportunities. He believed uniformity was one means to make that happen. To that end he (and the board) established that the "official" Bible that was to be used by all staff in all classes would be the New King James Version. There had been some minor grumbling about the autocratic nature of the decree, but none of the dissent lasted very long. Two days before parent/teacher conferences however, Nick Lansky came home from school and informed his father that Mr. Jasper, his science teacher, had put up a large bulletin board display in his room saying a different translation was better. This was what had Gerard Lansky steaming. Helen could hardly keep up as he briskly marched down the hall a few paces in front of her.

"Do me one favor," she asked reaching for his arm to slow him down.

"What's that?"

"At least let him explain before you bite his head off."

"I'm not going to bite his head off. He is going to take that thing down right in front of me or I am going to fire him on the spot."

"That's the way it is, is it? You, the big Christian man, going to do no listening, going to show no mercy. Oh, by the way. He doesn't work for you. He works for the board. This isn't one of your businesses Gerry."

This was that argument Helen had been saving for later. When she had to, she could really tell it like it was.

"OK. I'll hear what he has to say. But that thing is coming down, tonight! You cannot allow employees to defy you. If you do, your business will crumble."

"I thought this was a school?" she added dryly.

"Arrgh."

When the Lansky's entered the room, Mr. Jasper was seated at his desk. The offending bulletin board was directly behind him. The background was light gray bordered in a red trim. "The Best Translation of the Bible is the R and D Version" was emblazoned in an arc shape, centered across the top, in bold blue letters. Underneath the statement was a representation of a huge Bible with R&D on the cover.

"Why did you put that bulletin board up there?" Gerard blurted out. His terse tone ramped up the tension in the room instantly. No one had even had a chance to sit down yet.

"I wanted to talk with the students about this version."

"Well I don't know who you think you are to decide for this school that your version is superior to all others. I want that thing down. I want it down now! I haven't even heard of the R&D version before. What is it? Some revised something or other?"

"No sir," Mr. Jasper responded. The R&D Version is the Reading and Doing Version. Surely there is no better translation than that?"

Gerard Lansky stood motionless. His blank expression looked like an idiotic mask. And he was silent; a rare occurrence for him. All the wind had leaked out of his sails. He wanted to say something. He wanted to say something real bad, but he couldn't.

Helen started laughing.

"I think we can go home now," she chuckled.

She drove this time.

The twenty-minute ride home was stone silent.

"Well?" Helen turned toward him after she parked in the driveway.

"Well what?"

She gave him her best "raised eyebrow" glare.

"I'll stop by and apologize to him tomorrow."

"And?"

"I'll revoke that KJV thing also."

Helen smiled. "Thank you."

She leaned over and kissed him on the forehead.

"Whoever exalts himself will be humbled."

Matthew 23:12

Broken Hearted

The old man inside the cavernous vault watched as the thousand pound door slowly closed. He felt the pressure change in his ears when the seal was secured. He was not alone. The others with him also watched the door close and felt the darkness engulf them. No one spoke. Two women sharing a shawl, huddled together arms clasped, forehead-to-forehead. One of the younger men paced, his worn leather sandals were silent on the floor. The others sat by themselves with their backs pressed against the windowless wall. Two small oil lamps glowing softly spread enough light so the old man could see as he reached for his wife's hand. Together, they sat on a woolen blanket spread out over a heaping pile of loose straw.

Outside, the sky cracked and there were loud rumbles, like giant boulders crashing into each other. All these sounds were foreign to the little troupe. One especially loud boom caused the pacing to stop and pushed the two huddled women even closer. The others nervously shifted their positions. The man's wife squeezed his hand and pulled his arm to her side. He returned the hug, embracing her and whispering reassurances. Gently, he released his arms and went over to a ladder lashed to the side of a thick towering post. He climbed, and climbed some more. When he reached the turret-like cubicle at the top, he peered out a small opening in the upper part of one wall. The sky was dark and swirling. The wind was stirring. He saw water falling from the sky. It splashed on the planks of the endless deck. Leaves swayed on the trees below as monstrous raindrops bandied them about. The man looked off into the distance. As he feared, they were coming. Some running, others were riding camels or being carried on wagons pulled by various farm animals. Most were frantically waving their hands.

Despite the rain and thunder, he could hear what the people were yelling. Some were screaming his name.

Many were shrieking.

"Stop!"

"Wait!"

"Help us!"

He recognized his neighbors and a few close friends. His uncle and cousins were the first to start pounding on the walls. Then he saw his older sister. She spied him in his little window and began pleading with him to open the door. He couldn't take any more. He looked away and almost choked as convulsing sobs racked his body.

Soon there were hundreds surrounding the wood beamed titan, pounding and demanding access. Some tried in vain to swing ropes with large hooks to the upper deck with hopes of scaling the sheer walls. The deck was too high. One group actually cut down a tree and leaned it against one of the enormous faces, but they broke out into a fight as they climbed over each other on the trunk. Then the rain intensified. Sheets of water poured down so heavily the man could no longer see out his little window. He carefully made his way down the ladder. All the animals were silent as the man made his way through each deck. Lions and elephants bowed their heads in reverence. Horses and cattle were at rest. Two bears started into hibernation. The sheep came and rubbed their heads against his leg. Doves covered their nests without a coo and the dogs neither barked nor whined.

When the man got back down to his family it was obvious that they too had heard the pounding and screaming. His son's tried to be stoic, but the man could see that they were shaken and their wives were now a huddled trio. He sat by his own wife and placed his arm around her shoulder as she covered her ears in a futile attempt to block out the agonizing cries. He closed his eyes and hung his head as wave after wave of pain washed over him. Just as his friends and loved ones outside were helpless to stop the torrential tide rising upon them, the man could not stop the overwhelming flood of hurt crashing through his heart.

In anguish, the man cried out to God.

In doing so, he came to understand. God's heart was breaking too. Their suffering was shared.

"All flesh that moved on the earth perished, birds and cattle and beasts and every swarming thing that swarms upon the earth, and all mankind; of all that was on dry land, all in whose nostrils was the breath of life, died."

Genesis 7:21-22

The List

Ernest Lawson had been an elder at Edgewater Bible Church for almost 30 years. He served on the board faithfully and consistently looked out for the needs of the less fortunate. He could always be counted on when the call went out for clean up or fix up projects. He served communion, was a greeter, and a generous financial supporter. He fulfilled his role with all solemnity and was truly an honest man. His calm and reassuring manner earned him the respect of many. Although meetings were what he disliked the most about being an elder, he dutifully attended them, even the large congregational meetings, which he enjoyed the least.

"Too many people droning on and on, about issues that are already settled," he would complain to his wife.

Tonight's meeting had only one agenda item. As he drove to the church he started to feel a bit defensive. EBC had a long-standing, official code of conduct. It contained the usual: don't drink, don't smoke, don't chew, and don't associate with those that do, as well as entertainment and recreation restrictions. If a person wanted to become a member of EBC, they had to sign this contract with its list of seven "I will not" statements. Although all signed, few adhered. It was common practice in the church to tell prospective members that it was just a formality, not something to be concerned about. Sign it and forget it. However, there were a few members who wanted to confront the hypocrisy and put an end to the code. That is why Ernest was feeling defensive. He had been one of the original drafters of the code of conduct. He was proud of the moral stance the code represented. He was sure it was what kept EBC on the right track. It was the church's way of confronting the moral decay of the world. It enabled EBC to stand in stark contrast to the laxness

25

of some of the other churches in town.

There were well over a hundred people seated in the small sanctuary when Ernest arrived. It wasn't too hard to get a feel of what people in the church thought about the issue; for the most part they were seated in their own camps on either side of the center aisle.

The pastor opened the meeting with a brief prepared statement on why they were gathered and then offered a perfunctory prayer. It didn't take long for the discussion to heat up. People from both sides of the argument passionately expressed their views. There wasn't much listening. For the most part, people were impatiently waiting their turn to speak. There were frequent interruptions and the tone of the dialogue lost politeness early on.

Ernest bid his time. After he was confident that the discussion points had been thoroughly exhausted, he stood up and cleared his throat.

"I have been a member of this church for 35 years," he began. "This isn't the first time our stance on holiness has been under fire. And I am sure it will not be the last. Maybe some of you here who don't agree with our commitment to discipleship, would be better suited in another church setting. The code is our foundation here at Edgewater Bible Church."

One of the more vocal members of the opposition responded.

"Ernest, are you saying this list of do's and don'ts is the foundation of our church? I thought Jesus was the foundation of the church?"

He held a copy of the conduct code up in the air as he spoke.

"Do you realize that because of what Jesus did at Cana, He couldn't be a member of this church?"

Ernest ignored the Jesus membership comment. Besides, every serious Bible student knew it was really grape juice and not wine, despite the headwaiters praise for the groom.

"God commanded us to be Holy. We need to take a moral stand to keep from becoming a wayward assembly. I don't think

26

any of us want that to happen."

The vote was close.

On the way home Earnest took no small amount of comfort that once again he had turned back the tide of the less committed from watering down the tenets of his church.

"If you have died with Christ to the elementary principles of the world, why as if you were still in the world do you submit yourself to decrees such as, 'Do not handle, do not taste, do not touch!' in accordance with the commandments and teachings of men? These matters which have, to be sure, the appearance of wisdom in self-made religion and self abasement and severe treatment of the body, but are of no value against fleshly indulgence."

Colossians 2:20-23

Even in the Little Things

Brennan Manning, one of my most revered authors, says that the real difference between Christians today is not catholic vs. protestant, not charismatic vs. dispensational, not liberal vs. conservative. Rather, he suggests, the real difference is between those who are aware and those who are not. I am sure we can agree that all of us would benefit from a little more awareness.

In Minnesota, the second weekend in May is beyond momentous. Hundreds of thousands of men, women, and children migrate to the "lake" for the opening of fishing. Attire can range from long underwear and snowmobile suits, to light jackets, t-shirts, and jeans. Weather always dictates clothing but seldom the turnout. Hundreds of millions of dollars are spent on rods, reels, lures, bait, boats, electronics, food, beverage, and lodging. The ice is off the water (almost everywhere) and spirits are high. SUV's and pick-up trucks are pulling boats of all sizes and brands. Vehicles start clogging the main arteries heading north, days in advance. Many head to the big waters: Mille Lacs, Vermillion, Leech, Cass, and Winnie competing not only for the hot "spot" on the lake, but parking at access ramps as well. Others prefer smaller, more remote locations where the hope of solitude is as big a draw as the walleyes.

My dad and I have fished the opener together for years. This year we decided on going smaller and more remote. He had fished this particular lake years earlier, and always wanted to give it another try. I had not been on it before, but was willing to give it a go. We stopped for gas and minnows a few miles from the lake. Gas station/bait shop combinations are a common sight in northern Minnesota. If we have 10,000 lakes we have 20,000 gas station/bait shops. This town had two to choose from. We chose the one that looked the busiest.

One of the locals pulled up on the other side of the pump in his old beater F-150. He looked to be in his early eighties. His coat was starting to fray at the cuffs. He hadn't shaved in a few days and he had been faithfully wearing his sweat stained cap for some time.

"Going fishin'?" he asked after he slid the nozzle into the side of his truck.

My boat and trailer must have given me away.

"What lake are you going to?"

I was finished gassing up and I was in a bit of a hurry. We were running behind schedule the way it was and I didn't really want to get into a long conversation. However, I didn't want to be rude either.

"Pine Mountain," I finally answered.

"Haven't fished that lake for years. So I can't really give any pointers. But I know historically that shiners (type of minnow) work well early in the year."

"Uh huh."

"Have you fished it before?" he continued.

"Once many years ago."

"You have to be careful when you first head out on that lake."

"Why's that"?

"The new landing is in a nice little protected channel. But where the channel empties out to the lake there are submerged boulders and if you're not careful you can wreck your prop."

I started thinking this guy must really be living in the past. The landing is run by the Department of Natural Resources. They wouldn't leave submerged boulders unmarked.

My dad finally came out the door of the store.

"Thanks for the advice," I said nodding. "Nice talkin' to ya."

He answered with an ever so slight hunch of his shoulders and a casual wave of his hand.

The landing and the channel were on Pine Mountain's east side. There was a stiff breeze that day from the west rolling in waves that roiled the entrance to the lake, making navigation and boat control a little tricky.

There were no buoys.

Maybe the old guy was right.

I set my throttle at its lowest click and tipped up my prop. It wouldn't hurt to go easy.

Although the choppy water made visibility difficult, I counted eight jagged boulders. They were just below the surface and my hull barely cleared them as we eased on by. I looked at my lake map for the first place that we had decided to try. It was straight north. I then realized if I had not listened to the man at the gas station I would have taken an immediate right when I cleared the channel and full throttled my way right into the hidden rocks. Instead of starting off my season with a few tasty walleyes, I would have had a thousand dollar repair bill and never have wet my line.

Finally. Finally. I became aware. Aware that back at the gas station I had been totally unaware, dense. You could have called me Balaam.

I smiled.

I whispered a soft, "Thank you Jesus."

By the way, the old man was right about the shiners too.

"But the very hairs of your head are all numbered."

Matthew 10:30

God
Give me ears to hear.
There seems to be a waxy build up.
Teach me awareness.
I blow through life's moments
Senseless.
Proffer me the wisdom of reflection.
Haste and hurry litter my path.
Expand my vision
The material world is blocking my view.

31

The Balloon

Couldn't have been more than three or four. She had red hair, cheeks bursting with freckles and big green eyes. They were alert, intelligent eyes. With one hand she was holding a tiger face helium balloon and with the other, she was reaching up and hanging on to the pinky finger of an older gentleman. They were standing in front of the giraffes.

As often happens with a child and an untethered balloon, she let go of the string. Surprisingly, the little girl didn't whine or cry. Instead she turned her face upward, simply looking on with wonder as the balloon glided aloft.

She pointed one of her tiny fingers into the air and said, "Look Grandpa."

He did look. Although he wanted to, he wasn't quite able to look with childlike eyes. His acumen for business was too deeply ingrained. He had already calculated the material costs and park access fees of the balloon-man and his possible daily profit and compared that to his own income. He was aware of the pressurized gas in the tank needed to fill the balloon as well as the manufacture, function, and structure on the valves of the tank. He even knew the intricacies of how the helium was originally isolated and extracted from the atmosphere. He understood the differences in the density of gases and where helium registered on the periodic table of elements according to its atomic mass. He was well versed in solar radiation's effects on air currents and updrafts. He was aware of the low permeability of Mylar and the diffusion rate of helium across that membrane. He contemplated the chilling and subsequent condensing of the helium in the upper layers of the atmosphere, the balloon's loss of buoyancy, and its eventual descent back to earth. He knew that someday, somewhere, that balloon was going to be litter.

He was also cognizant of the fact that for the child, it was simply: "I opened my hand. I released the balloon. I watched it fly and it was fun." This brought great joy to the man. After all, he bought the balloon to give her joy.

He stopped watching the balloon and instead focused on the little girl holding his finger. He contemplated telling the girl where the balloon was going.

As the man pondered this moment it dawned on him how silly it would be for him to try to explain to the child all he knew about the science and economics of helium balloons. It would be beyond the child's understanding. It wouldn't enrich the child's experience. It would probably diminish it. It surely would have no impact on the flight of the balloon. Why, these thoughts would be farther over the child's head than the balloon itself.

The balloon soared to great and distant heights until it became an invisible dot in the far away sky.

When the balloon finally disappeared the child looked up at the man. There was an innocent smile of contentment on her face; that kind of smile only little children can produce.

The man smiled back. He squeezed her hand, swept her up in his arms and planted his nose and lips deep in her cheek.

Later, the two were seen again. Now they were in front of the polar bears. The girl had another balloon. It was tied around her wrist.

"For My thoughts are not your thoughts, Nor are your ways My ways, declares the Lord. For as the heavens are higher than the earth, So are My ways higher than your ways And My thoughts than your thoughts."

Isaiah 55:8-9

First Time

I was an extra hyper twelve-year old with no impulse control, devious thought patterns, and a mindless audacity to carry out unkind schemes. As you can imagine teachers loved me, especially Sunday school teachers. I usually didn't last a full class period. I spent many a Sunday morning outside the door in the hallway. I blurted out a stupid question, insulted a girl, or told the teacher what I thought about her flannel board characters. I never could figure out why Sunday after Sunday my parents would imprison me in a small room with small furniture where some old lady talked to us like two-year olds, telling us stories that she herself didn't believe actually happened. I never got straight answers for my questions either. "Who did Adam's kids marry?" "How come the animals came two by two?" "What is the story of David and Bathsheba all about?" "Did Judas kill himself or fall in some sharp stones?" "If Jesus was God why did he have to pray?" Not having any meaningful answers to my questions further fueled my unacceptable behavior. I zealously defended my stance of defiant rebellion to my religious incarceration, no matter what the consequences.

However.

One Sunday I did last the whole class period. We had a substitute. It was Carrie Snow's mom. She said she wasn't going to tell Bible stories. We wouldn't have to do crafts, or recite verses. She was going to talk to us about prayer.

She was different and right away her serene demeanor held my attention.

Nevertheless, I was a bit confused. Prayer was what the robed reverend did in front of the church. Prayer was a monotone congregational choral reading from a book that smelled old when you opened it. Prayer was what my grandfather did before the Thanksgiving meal. I sure hoped she wasn't going to talk about that.

"I am always alone when I pray." Mrs. Snow began. "I quiet myself and wait until I know He is in the room with me. I need to sense Him with me before I start talking with Him. I don't stop praying until I know He has heard me. Only then do I have peace."

That's all she said.

I shivered.

Goose bumps covered my arms and the hair went up on the back of my neck. My mouth was dry and I could literally feel my pulse. I know it was just Mrs. Snow talking, but somehow her words seemed like they were more than words. I was hearing them through more places than my ears. Something awakened inside of me, something I had never felt before. Her words were going straight to that new place.

It was my first time.

It was the first time I realized God was real.

It was the first time I learned that there was someone who knew God and actually talked to Him.

It was the first time that I wanted to know God too.

"But when you pray, go into your inner room, close your door and pray to your Father who is in secret, and your father who sees what is done in secret will reward you."

Matthew 6:6

Penn Station

One summer I took part in a demonstration in New York City that was to coincide with a large political convention. The national leaders of the denomination I was attending at the time had organized the event. Over four thousand people traveled from varying regions of the country to participate. Some churches sent bus loads, others caravaned, and still others came by train or plane. Many individuals sacrificed personal finances to participate in this rally that was going to "impact the public square" for righteousness.

The organizers were quite adept at administrative details. They had rented dorms at a New Jersey university, chartered a special train to take us back and forth into the city for the rally, and secured a prime location outside Madison Square Garden where we would make our proclamations. Because we had obtained the proper permits, the police even blocked off the street for us. Our demonstration and political action statements about Christian values and the loss of morality in Washington made Newsweek, the New York Times, and the local TV affiliates. In our youthful exuberance we really thought we had done, "something for God."

Upon reflection, probably the only thing we did for God was give Him a headache. Somewhere, someplace, someone got the idea that a large group of Christians, shouting rhetoric and carrying signs on the streets of New York City would really have a positive spiritual impact on the political machine. Do you ever look back on some of the convictions you had as your younger self and cringe?

However, after all our grandstanding was done, there was a genuine God thing that happened that actually did have an impact. Just before we were to board our trains for Jersey, our entire throng was in the main lobby at Penn Station when we were told that our departure was delayed approximately twenty minutes. They didn't want us down by the tracks. We were told to remain in the main lobby of the station. Since there were so many of us we couldn't easily find places to sit. We just stood there dispersed throughout the station. A group of about 30 or so started singing a chorus familiar to all of us from the last two verses of Jude:

Now to Him who is able to keep you
Who is able to keep you from stumbling
And to make you stand in His presence
Of His glory blameless with great joy.
To the only God our Savior
Through Jesus Christ our Lord
Be glory majesty dominion and power
Before all time now and forever.
Before all time now and forever.

As others of our group heard, they joined. Before the chorus had been sung the second time we were four thousand voices strong, a cappella, resounding off the cavernous ceilings of the iconic station. While we sang the chorus through two or three more times, the miraculous happened. For about thirty seconds everything and everyone in Penn Station stopped. No ticket transactions, no bustling to a departure, no one folding a paper, no children whining, no voices over the loudspeaker, not a foot step heard, not a door creaked, not a wheel squeaked. Even the shoeshine men stopped hawking. Every living soul simply stopped and listened. Some bowed their heads, others stared at the oddity, and still others quietly closed their eyes and let the heavenly reverberation wash over them. When we stopped singing there was a peaceful silence and a heavy, feelable, almost touchable, invisible something in the air. For a few seconds we were all under the power of the pause button. Gradually, and with noticeably muted voices, people went back to their routines and destinations. It took almost two minutes for Penn Station to get back to its customary roar.

A middle aged black woman had been standing next to me as we sang. She reached into her purse and pulled out some tissues. She dabbed her eyes and wiped her cheeks. When we were finished she took a step closer. She placed her hand on my arm.

"Thank you," she whispered.

"O Thou art holy, Thou who inhabits the praises of His people."
Psalm 22:3

Stemming the Tide

In Spruce Ridge, high school baseball is huge. Out of control huge. Most college teams don't play on fields as nice as Titan Field. On road trips the team travels on a custom fitted, air-conditioned bus with the Titan logo emblazoned on both sides. They eat at the finest restaurants the away team's town has to offer. All is paid for by the baseball "fund." The local paper has two columns in the Thursday edition dedicated entirely to covering Titan baseball. The local radio station's Saturday morning programming is a baseball call in show. Some of the better players are laden with minor celebrity status. Fathers will stop them on the street to sign autographs for their young sons. They pass all their classes, deservedly or not. A player will regularly be handed "coupons" for free pizza, free ice cream, and free go-carts. At least once a month a starter will attend a service club luncheon where the food is great and the baseball chats are sprinkled with pats on the back and promises of leisurely summer employment. The occasional traffic violation never garners a ticket. A visit by a college recruiter or professional scout always feeds breakfast conversations at the local cafés. And of course, there were the games themselves. A packed house was guaranteed, replete with tailgating, profitable concessions, and everyone clad in Titan Gear.

However, . . . the Spruce Ridge Titans had a dark, tightly held, decades old secret. A ritualistic hazing that happened once a year, every year. In the shadowy circles of those in the know, it had grown to be dubbed, "Tomato Torture." It always happened on the way home from the Harding trip. Even though Harding was almost three hours away, they were the Titan's fiercest rivals. Part of the hoopla surrounding the weekend series was to make both days a double header with the freshman teams playing the preliminary game. The freshman took a separate bus (A regular school bus. Not

41

air-conditioned.). However, each year a few upper classmen would feign friendship to one of the freshman and make him feel wanted. He was hand picked. He either: mouthed off to the wrong person, talked to someone's girlfriend, wandered into the varsity locker room, or was simply disliked. He was always a bench player. The prospective victim would receive an "invitation" to ride back home on the varsity bus. With the cover of night's darkness he would be brought to the back of the bus where he would be forced to the floor and pinned down at the wrists and ankles. Countless rotten tomatoes would be stuffed between his clothing and every square inch of his skin. Then they would be squished with fist blows that were never gentle. His cap would be filled with tomato mush and wrestled onto his head. In less than ten minutes he was a wet, bruised, sticky mess. If the physical humiliation weren't enough, all the while he was being pummeled, he would be told what people really thought of him. As a closing act there was a solemn warning. If he made a big deal of the incident, he might as well move to another town. The crowning blow? The victim still had more than two hours sitting in the presence of his predators. For most sufferers, it was the end of their baseball participation.

Of course, a long standing, carefully cloaked tradition like this cannot go on year after year without coaches and other adults plugging their ears, closing their eyes, and turning their heads. Boys will be boys and all that; survival of the fittest.

This year's victim was Calvin Macready. His vanity and naiveté made him easy to seduce. After the game two seniors, Jared Wahkon and Benny Carter were walking him back to the bus, all smiles, making Calvin feel important. They were just about to board when Travis Settles the student equipment manager was standing in the steps.

They don't come more non-athletic than Travis. Thick glasses, white socks, tucked in button down shirts, and pants that were an inch too short made him the poster child for Nerds R Us. For most of the players, conversations with Travis consisted of: "Travis get this," "Travis where is my…" or "Travis did you bring the…?" He was never invited to parties and he didn't sit with the team at lunch. On top of that, someone saw him reading a Bible once, ensuring him eternal "outsider" status.

Today for some reason, there he stood, arms folded, blocking entrance to the bus.

"Excuse us Travis." Jared ordered, implying he better move.

He didn't.

"Excuse us Travis." He repeated with even more emphasis. "Hard of hearing today?"

"Don't bring him on the bus." Travis said flatly, nodding toward Calvin.

"Out of the way." Both the players took a step closer. Jared gave Travis a push.

He still didn't move.

Calvin was oblivious.

"You will have to go through me." Travis stated.

They both laughed. "That won't be too hard."

Then Travis spoke directly to Calvin. "These two aren't your friends. They plan on hurting you tonight on the way home. You should run and get on that ninth grade bus right now."

"Shut up Travis!" Jared and Benny grunted in unison.

Calvin finally wised up and tried to escape. Benny tightly gripped his arms. Calvin wouldn't be the first hazing victim to be dragged onto the bus.

Travis backed up one step. His grip tightened on both handrails.

Jared walked right up to Travis, nose to nose, acting all macho with his toughest glare. He was totally unprepared, however, for what happened next.

There is a common theme in the traditions of many cultures about someone's eyes, a belief they are a window to the soul. If a person can actually see through that window, it only takes a moment for the contents revealed. Jared was granted a peek through Travis' windows and when he did, he witnessed it all. It was more than he bargained for. There was courage, character, and resolve. There was a fortified personal conviction of right and a willingness to sacrifice for it. The manifestation brought him to a halt.

What shook him even more was that he saw himself also. He was someone who got entertainment from the humiliation of others. He had never sacrificed anything for anyone, and right was what ever was convenient and self-serving at the time. He had not considered the feelings of others once in his entire life.

It was a revelation. It was a crossroads moment.

Travis was a young man with a giant inside of him. Jared was an irresponsible, selfish little boy. In the whole of his young life, he had never felt so lacking, so small, so convicted.

Jared stepped back and turned toward Benny.

"Let him go."

"What…?" Benny protested.

"It's not worth it."

"What are you talking about?"

"Just let him go."

Benny was confused and ticked, but he was a follower and usually did what Jared told him.

"You're lucky kid." Benny sneered at Calvin as he gave him a shove in the back.

Travis didn't leave his post until Calvin was on the freshman bus.

Tomato Torture never again reared its ugly head in Titan land. A longstanding, mean spirited hazing tradition unceremoniously came to a close with four slightly confused young boys unsure about what had just transpired between them.

By chance, years later Jared and Travis ran into each other at a coffee shop. Unbeknownst to each other, they both lived in the same city only blocks apart. They sat together and talked about the incident at Harding. Jared had come to a stage in his life where he wanted to know why Travis bothered to intervene.

"Despite my protests," Travis began. "My mother required me to participate in an extra-curricular activity. Since I liked statistics, I chose baseball. I found out about Tomato Torture on the ride home from the previous year's trip to Harding. I was horrified. From that night on I knew the Lord was impressing on me that I had a purpose for being the student manager that was more than keeping accurate box scores. I realized I needed to stop the hazing, but I had no idea how. It plagued me the entire year. I was so panicked about being the one to intervene that I begged my mother to let me quit the baseball team. She refused. As the Harding trip drew closer, I argued with God daily. The morning of the trip I faked like I was sick. I wasn't good enough at faking to fool my mom."

"Travis," she finally said. "I know that there is something about this baseball thing that is really bothering you and I know you won't tell me what it is. Let me just say one thing. Courage is not the absence of fear. It is doing what you know is right in the midst of the fear."

"For we are His workmanship, created in Christ Jesus for good works, which God prepared beforehand so that we would walk in them."

Ephesians 2:10

Drifting

Lord

I am drifting.
Be the great anchor with Your keeping and holding power.

I am drifting and listing.
Be the lighthouse on the cape
Keeping my keel from the rocky shoals.

I am drifting, listing, and windswept.
Be the great rudder steering true,
Be the unbreakable mast against the raging storm.

I am drifting.
I am listing.
I am windswept and I am empty.
Be the North Star, shimmering brightly,
Pointing out the heavenly way.
Bring me to a mooring of safe haven
Where waters run cool and deep.
Repair my riggings, secure my hull, laden my decks.
Chart a path for me through purposeful seas
To ports of call that fulfill my Captain's bidding.

The Pink Elevator

Dreams are a mysterious venture of the mind and spirit. To the scientist they are merely electrochemical interactions ignited by recent events or possibly spicy food. To the spiritualist, dreams are a symbolic portal to the divine, where life-guiding messages can be derived from the slightest detail. Although most of us aren't willing to affix ourselves firmly to either of those extremes, we still experience and wonder about our dreams. Maybe it doesn't have to be either/or? Why can't some dreams be the result of a bad day followed by too many jalapeños while others are a deposit from the Spirit? I've had my share of dreams where the flow of events are crazy and the details are fuzzy, fading soon after I wake. I've also had dreams where all the specifics remain clear years afterward. As much as I've tried not to attach too much meaning to them, there is meaning and I know it.

From the early patriarchs to John on Patmos, dreams have been part of the God experience. It was a dream that provided Joseph a "get out of jail free" card and an audience with Pharaoh. Through a dream, Mary's Joseph came to know of the purity of his young fiancé and important details of his future course. It was a dreamlike trance that allowed Peter to understand that God wanted all peoples to know of His love, not just the Hebrews. It probably wouldn't be wise to bet the house on a message we feel we've derived from a dream. It might not be wise to utterly dismiss them either.

Sometimes dreams even have a pink elevator.

It was an idyllic summer evening with the last peek at the sun just moments away. A neighborhood park in a big city was full of people milling about enjoying the cool evening breezes and the long shadows from the ancient oaks and elms. I was wearing camouflaged military garb complete with boots and helmet. I was sprinting and dodging my way through the park toward the front entry of a large upscale hotel, circa 1920's. Someone was shooting at me. I didn't know from where or why bullets were buzzing by my head. One eventually tore through my sleeve, burning my skin as it grazed my arm. The park patrons were oblivious to the gunfire and looked up at me with quizzical expressions as I streaked by. Out of the corner of my eye I noticed there were two others rolling and weaving and running the same direction as I. When I broke out between two parked cars to cross the street I was hit in the back. I staggered and went down. Somehow I was able to lurch and drag myself to the front door. Just before the entrance I was hit again.

My dad was there. He too was wearing military clothing.

I died in his arms.

Wordlessly he dragged my body across the lobby. The elevator doors were decorated with an ornate design of heavy brass and bronze. They were a creative touch to the grand architectural design of the hotel. The doors opened and my dad pulled me inside. He left me there alone on the floor and went back to the front door. As the elevator made its ascent the walls began to dissolve and the floor turned into a giant pink disk. When I reached the top an enormous playground lay before me in the midst of a lush green expanse. There were swing sets, complex jungle gyms, and slides so high that you couldn't tell if the next person in line was a boy or a girl. Children dressed in bright colored clothing were playing ball, jumping rope, sailing boats, climbing trees, flying kites and making frequent visits to picnic tables. Tables that were covered in shimmering tablecloths and endless platters heaped to overflowing with every delicious food imaginable. Every time someone reached into one of the blue coolers at the end of a table they pulled out a perfectly stacked triple scoop ice cream cone. There was laughter and shouts of joy at a goal scored or a remote control plane making a perfect landing. Music wasn't exactly playing. It was in the atmosphere. Many melodies flowing all at once somehow blending into a harmonious overture with a rhythm that wouldn't stop percolating through your toes. Bright red birds, deep blue birds, and birds of a color I had never seen flitted overhead. A splendid variety of animals roamed the grounds and every once and a while a silvery fish would break the surface of the water in a perfect arc. The only adult was a woman of matronly proportions. She wore a dusky blue smock with an off white apron. Her thick brown hair was pulled back into a ponytail with a red ribbon. I couldn't tell how old she was. 30? 60? Ageless? And her background was a mystery too. Asian? African? European? Middle Eastern? It was none of them and all of them.

I walked toward her.

When she saw me approaching she turned slightly my way and smiled.

"Welcome."

How could she be so much taller than me?

I examined myself. I had become a child like all the rest. My bullet wounds were gone. My fatigues replaced by a light cotton shirt, baggy shorts, and tennis shoes.

She reached out her hand and tousled my hair.

"Many of your friends are here. Play wherever you like and don't forget to eat."

I joined a soccer game on the other side of a lazy stream. One of the girls kicked the ball over my head. As I chased it down, it kept rolling. It was only then that I noticed the green expanse did not go on forever. It was slightly elevated and had a border made of landscape timbers. The ball rolled off the edge down a slight embankment and came to rest against the base of a dead tree.

Outside the border there were no lawns or living trees. Everything was cast in shades of dull gray. Not one note of music, flight of a bird, or a sound of laughter was to be found. The sky was overcast and the chilling air had a faint smell of rotten eggs. The buildings were in sore need of paint. Their windows had an oily smudgy coating, and all the porches had broken railings and missing steps. As I looked closer I noticed there were some people after all. They were kids too. Only a few, and they stood off at a distance. Their clothes were dark and their faces downward cast as

51

they listlessly shuffled about with hands in their pockets. A small group started walking to the tree where the ball lay. One of them picked it up and kicked it my way. It bounced at my feet. I waved for them to come and join me.

One of the older boys did walk toward me. He stopped a few feet from the border as if coming closer wasn't allowed. He lifted his face. His black eyes held an ancient, weary sorrow.

"Come and play soccer with us," I suggested.

"We can't."

The very moment he spoke the matron was at my side. She held me firmly at her hip until the anguish finished spilling out of me.

She clasped my hand and we walked silently back to the soccer field.

"And besides all this, between us and you there is a great chasm fixed, so that those who wish to come over from here to you will not be able, and none may cross over from there to us."

Luke 16:26

The High Dive

There is a small community in the Upper Midwest called Breaker Point situated on the southern boundary of what is commonly known as the lake country. The city has operated a public swimming beach on Pleasant Lake for over 40 years. It has 200 feet of sugar sand shoreline that is groomed daily. The backdrop of majestic pines and spacious grounds, combined with exceptionally clear water makes "the beach" as it is known locally, a popular destination. The city also prides itself for having a perfect safety record. There has been a close call or two over the years, but never a drowning or even a serious injury. For two recent summers Brandon Royal and Charlie Hite have been the head lifeguards. It was their "home from college for the summer" job. They took it seriously. There would be no harm coming to anyone on their watch, which was noon to 8:00 p.m. six days a week.

One particular Sunday morning they arrived earlier than usual. Two women were already out on the diving raft, which was about 100 feet from shore. They were waving, and screaming, and pointing to the water. Amidst their incoherent shrieks Brandon did hear the word "drowning." He quickly jumped on the life board and paddled furiously to where the girls were pointing. Charlie phoned 911 and soon followed in the rowboat. When Brandon closed in, he saw a man suspended a couple of feet below the surface, motionless. His skin was a pale bluish white. Brandon was sure he was already dead. Regardless, he reached down, grabbed him by the hair, and pulled his head above the water. He paddled over to the raft and hoisted the dead weight onto the deck. He ordered the girls to stop screaming. Then he turned the body face down, applied some pressure, and was able to force out a little water. He rolled the man back over and started CPR. The first repetitions yielded no response. He intensified his efforts.

Finally there was a spasm, then a cough. Brandon rolled him over again. He vomited into the water. When he was sure no more was coming, Brandon sat him up and had him sit quietly. Charlie helped the man, still woozy, into the rowboat. When they got back to shore, the police and the ambulance were already waiting. The EMT's took the man to the hospital for observation.

Brandon got the story from the young women. The three of them had been out drinking and partying all night and into the morning. Manfred "Manny" Plains bragged that when he was younger he had been a competitive diver and that he could still go off the high board. The boasting led to a challenge. Since no sober minds were involved, the three inebriates were soon swimming out to the raft ignoring all warning signs to the contrary. The first couple of dives if not artistic were at least injury free. However, on his final attempt his foot slipped to one side of the diving board. He fell, hitting his head soundly on the way down. He crashed to the water and gradually drifted a few yards from the raft. Once the girls realized he wasn't faking, the screaming commenced.

Word of mouth spreads fast in small towns. Stories of how "Manny the drunk" had been saved were soon on the lips of most Breaker Point residents. For their part, Brandon and Charlie didn't have much to say. Privately, they were grateful they had been able to save him and yet a little mystified that he had never contacted them to offer thanks or talk about what had happened. Maybe he was embarrassed. Maybe he didn't know any better. Word was that Manny was not exactly a scholar.

The rest of the summer passed by uneventfully until the week before Brandon and Charlie were to head back to school. It was a Saturday night and they were planning on going to a midnight bonfire. Brandon had forgotten his phone at the lifeguard house, so they swung by the beach to pick it up. Heavy cloud cover made things darker than normal. Even so, upon getting out of the car they noticed someone standing out on the raft. They hurried down to the beach and headed out in the rowboat. When they got closer they recognized the late night swimmer.

"What are you doing out here Manny?" they asked.

"How do you guys know my name?"

"We're the ones who saved you a couple of months ago."

"Oh yeah. I probably never thanked you for that. Sorry. But you know what? They made me pay a fine for swimming after hours and pay for the ambulance call."

"So, what are you doing out here tonight then?" they asked again.

"Swimming."

"That's not such a good idea is it?" Brandon replied.

"Isn't that for me to decide?"

"You already know it's dangerous."

"I felt like doing some dives. There's no law against that."

"Well actually there is a law about being out here when no one is on duty."

"That's just some silly city ordinance. That's all about CYA."

"I guess that's your choice," Charlie finally chipped in.

"Planning on stopping me?"

"No, we'll just watch."

Manny climbed to the top of the diving tower. The placing of his feet on the ladder rungs were not exactly those of an agile athlete. He made one awkward dive off the high board. His landing was a combination belly flop head slap. It dazed him. He laid motionless on the surface. The boys maneuvered the boat a small distance away and watched. There was no struggle. He was face down with arms spread wide. A few minutes later he was sinking. When the boys were sure he wasn't coming back up, they quietly rowed back to shore and proceeded on with their late night plans.

The next day Ken Monson out for some early morning bass discovered Manny's body. A couple of bar patrons had heard him talking big a few nights earlier about how he wasn't going to let the city keep him from going off the high tower any time he wanted. Most folks in town surmised he got what was coming to him.

Brandon and Charlie figured they already saved him once. That should have been enough.

Allegory: 1. a representation of abstract or spiritual meaning by means of symbolic or fictional figures. 2. To speak figuratively 3. Figurative treatment of one subject under the guise of another.

"My sheep hear My voice, and I know them, and they follow Me: and I give eternal life to them, and they will never perish: and no one will snatch the out of My hand. My Father who has given them to Me is greater than all: and no one is able to snatch them out of the Father's hand. I and the Father are one."

John 10:27-30

Thoughts On Grace

Grace is not offered to those who deserve it.
If it were, by its very nature, it would no longer be grace.
And, of course, there are none deserving.
That's the thing about grace.
It is grace.

Maybe you have heard,
"If you don't live by a high enough standard all you have is cheap grace."
No.
Grace is not cheap. It is costly.
Cost beyond measure. The precious blood was not and is not cheap.
How do we even put a valuation on Jesus leaving His supernatural existence,
Becoming a man, and taking on the full brunt of God's wrath?

Want to cheapen grace?
Have the attitude that what you do is of equal or greater value than what Jesus did on the cross.
Then you will have reduced grace to the level of self-congratulations.
Worse yet, use someone's formula to "access" God's grace.
To make God's grace, "work for you."
Grace will then have been cheapened to the level of a twenty-five cent paperback on a table at a garage sale next to a rumpled beefcake romance novel.

Fall from grace?
Imagine your piety produces acceptance from God.
Believe your manner of "walking after God" is superior to those "Christmas and Easter only Christians."

Ignore the "righteousness of Christ" and believe in your own.
Live the illusion that God, or anyone else for that matter, is impressed
with your prayers, your good works, or your giving and you will be
living below grace.
You will have fallen from it.

The longer we live
The greater the realization grows,
Of our desperate need for grace
The greater the realization grows,
That grace answers everything.

Grace flows from the unfathomable deep that is God.
The great deep of His love
The great deep of His resources
The great deep of His compassion

Grace is planted firmly on the unshakable mountain that is God.
The mountain of His promise
The mountain of His character
The mountain of His will.

There is a great mystery and splendor surrounding grace.
It has value that is beyond calculation
Yet, it is free.
Accepting that mystery is a good first step
Toward walking in the grace in which we have been called.

"Therefore prepare your minds for action,
keep sober in spirit, fix your hope
completely on the grace to be brought
to you at the revelation of Jesus Christ."
1 Peter 1:13

Celebrity

Jimmy Barnes was a typical fifteen-year old, medium build, average height, wavy brown hair, and ruddy cheeks. He had an engaging smile that put others at ease and made him comfortable to be around. Sports, music, friends, and a part time job completed his routine outside of school. What may have made him somewhat atypical was that he went to church with his parents, willingly. He liked worship on Sunday mornings and was an active member of the youth group. One Sunday the pastor gave a presentation concerning different "jobs" in the church that needed filling. There were a few "openings" in the sound booth. Jimmy expressed his interest to the head of the sound ministry and after a few training sessions it was apparent that he was catching on quickly. In only a few short months he was a regular on the sound booth rotation.

The following spring, Jimmy's church was hosting an international evangelist for a series of meetings. The Saturday night meeting was advertised in the community as having a youth focus and would be held in the auditorium at the community center. Jimmy went and he managed to get a couple of his un-churched friends to join him.

When the big night arrived, the auditorium slowly began to fill with people of all ages, including plenty of young people. A couple of minutes after Jimmy and his friends found their seats he felt a tap on his shoulder. It was his pastor. The person assigned to do sound that evening had just called with a family emergency. Jimmy was getting his arm twisted to fill in. Doing sound at church with an experienced person close by was one thing. Running the sound at a community event in a sound booth he hadn't seen before, and by himself, was another matter altogether. He agreed, reluctantly.

The sound check went fine. The worship team started playing. Soon there was singing, clapping, and hands being raised. All was going well.

The evangelist arrived late. There was someone with him. The companion stopped by the sound booth and handed a cassette to Jimmy.

"Put it on side A," was all he said.

After the final worship song the evangelist informed the crowd that he had brought along a special musical guest. Quite a number of people knew who he was and gave him a rousing ovation. Jimmy didn't know who he was. He figured he must be important, however. His watch and rings were worth more money than Jimmy made at his part time job in a year.

The singer gave a discreet nod toward the booth and Jimmy pushed play. The tape was the type where there is music and vocals on one side and music only on the other. The music only side served as accompaniment for the singer. As the intro started to play, the guest singer held the microphone prayerfully at his breast. He closed his eyes and fashioned an often rehearsed, worshipful expression onto his face. The moment he opened his mouth to sing his first note, the vocals from the tape blared through the loudspeakers. His eyes opened with surprise. He glared at Jimmy.

"I said side A."

Jimmy looked again. It was on side A.

Before he could answer the singer spoke again.

"Turn it to the other side." The tension from his voice descended onto the audience from the speakers above.

The singer waited. He wasn't wearing his worshipful expression any more.

Jimmy was embarrassed. He was sure the eyes in the back of everyone's head were staring right at him. Because he was a little flustered he forgot to rewind the tape. When he pushed play it didn't start at the beginning.

The singer shot Jimmy a quick unpleasant glance and then turned toward the crowd. "I apologize," he said. "I am so used to working with professionals that…" He waved his hand toward the sound booth. "Well, you understand."

His comment generated a few nervous chuckles and forced smiles.

The rest of the crowd sat stoically.

As the tape rewound Jimmy felt his embarrassment growing. His cheeks were aflame and he was fighting valiantly to hold in his emotions. He did manage to give a sign when the tape was ready. The singer folded his hands and once again struck his worshipful pose.

When the song was over, the pastor, the evangelist, and the rest of the important attendees in the front row tried to lead a less than spirited audience in applause. Before the singer sat down in the chair that had been reserved for him, he reminded the people that he would have CD's for sale in the lobby after the meeting. The rest of evening went forward as planned.

When all was over, not one single person had a word of condolence or encouragement for young Jimmy. People simply pretended that nothing had happened.

On the car ride home however, Carl, one of Jimmy's friends faithfully pointed out, "Man that singer guy was really an a_ _ hole!"

Jimmy's smile was bittersweet.

Friends are the best, he thought to himself. *Not the first church experience I wanted for them though.*

"Do nothing from selfishness or empty conceit, but with humility of mind regard one another as more important than yourselves."
Philippians 2:3

Red Lake

I am standing on Red Lake
Nine miles from shore
2:00 a.m.
23 below zero, a tear freezes on my cheek
Snow squeaks beneath my boots
The crisp air is silent
I can almost hear my heart beat
Tonight the stars are not light years away
They are splashed out on the touchable dome
That is the sky
If I walked to the horizon
I could hold some of them in my hand
Many gently shimmer
Others twinkle
A few boldly blaze
No light from man diminishes their glory
A chill creeps up my coat
The warmth of my fish house beckons
But I cannot move
The sparkle of the universe holds me still
I lay on my back
I think of the native
Standing on this very ice centuries before
A resonating call from all my primeval ancestors
Pulls on me deeply
An awareness of my lineage flows within
I am small

I am alive
I am vulnerable
My life is a faint breath, an unheard whisper

"When I consider Your heavens,
the work of Your fingers,
The moon and the stars, which
You have ordained;
What is man that You take
thought of him,
And the son of man that
you care for him?"

Psalm 8:3-4

A Morsel

Do you have a prayer that you've been directing toward God
for years, even decades, a longstanding request rendering all other
prayers mute in comparison? Is it one of those burdens that you've
repeatedly tried "casting onto Him," only to have it come back
and settle on your shoulders time and time again? Do you need an
intervention that transcends the natural? Is rest impossible without
the supernatural movement of His hand? Have you wondered if
God is ignoring you, or doesn't care? Maybe you have concluded that
the deists are right; God is just an ancient watchmaker who got the
whole thing ticking while He seldom tinkers? Have you resolved that
the verse "Jesus is the same yesterday, today, and forever" is merely a
literary device? Have you found the theological "experts," don't help
because their "insights" are either, "God doesn't do that any more,"
or "You need to press in with more faith?" And of course there is
the always popular, "Sometimes God's answer is no."

Those answers are always a great help.

I already know my faith is weak. I'm fully aware of the great
big no. And I have not yet been able to succumb to the idea of a
dispassionate, disengaged, dispensational deity.

There is always arguing, somehow thinking reasoning skills will
convince Him to move? Or maybe you've been through a time
of giving up, laying your hands down in resignation and settling
for disappointment, only to find that doesn't work either because
although suppressed, your heartache remains. Your burden endures
and you're unable to surrender into accepting the status quo. So,
with a receding hope that is battered and bruised you plead again,
absolutely unsure what level of intervention, if any, will ever come
forth.

Trusting is difficult when one is unable to interpret His response.
Hope deferred truly does sicken the heart and numb the soul. The

Psalmists shared this anguish. And they continued to doggedly hurl their struggles at Him. Yet, after they had laid out their complaints, they seemed to come to some sense of resolution, a place of trust, by reminding themselves of the parts of God's character they were rock solid on. Even if it meant they wouldn't see their satisfaction until they reached the other side. (See Psalm 17:15) I do have enough faith, I hope, to believe that in the hereafter my burden will be lifted. But it does not change the fact that I still hope for the here and now.

There is a passage that has kept me clinging to the faintest hope for a yes in the today. Many times it has kept me from totally giving up on God parting the curtain. It is the scene between Jesus and the Syrophoenician woman with the demon-possessed daughter.

Even though she was in a foreign land amongst strangers, she had a burden she would not run away from and she was convinced she had come to the only one who could deliver her from her anguish. However, when she found Him, He ignored her. Not only did he ignore her, His followers tried convincing Him to send her away. Basically, "Get that noisy, crazy woman away from us. Her foaming at the mouth daughter too."

I don't believe that Jesus was actually calling her a dog as some have suggested. (Mark 7:27) Rather, using an analogy, He was simply asking her, "Why would you, a Canaanite come to me a Hebrew rabbi?" Her answer swept past the cultural/terrestrial Jesus and went straight to the eternal/cosmic Jesus. She deferred, unknowingly I'm sure, to the blessing received by Abraham in Genesis 22:18. "In your seed all the nations of the earth shall be blessed..." Her comment about the crumbs extended Jesus' analogy. She was saying to Him. "You must be more than just a Jewish prophet. You must be from the God of all. You must be from the God who has designs to bless and show mercy to more than just the children of Jacob. Surely, He intended there to be leftovers for the rest of us. Those crumbs would be more than enough for me."

Although at the beginning of her quest Jesus delayed His action, ultimately He did come to her rescue. He did part the curtain between the natural and supernatural and allowed the miracle to flow.

God.
Here I am, again.
I know you are the only one who can fulfill my request.
Doing this would be no more difficult for You than wiping a crumbly morsel
off a table.
I long for that morsel.

"But she came and began to bow down before Him, saying 'Lord, help me!' And He answered and said, 'It is not good to take the children's bread and throw it to the dogs.' But she said, 'Yes, Lord; but even the dogs feed on the crumbs which fall from their master's table.' Then Jesus said to her, 'O woman your faith is great. It shall be done for you as you wish."

Matthew 15:25-28

Out of the Closet

It all started when I was supposed to bring a case of beer and a liter of bourbon home to my woman on a Friday night. I don't know if "home" is really the right word. The apartment actually belongs to her and I only stay there on weekends. "My woman" is not an accurate phrase either. She is someone who lets me sleep on her couch, take a shower, and keep a change of clothes at her place as long as I bring enough for both of us to drink. As we are both quiet drunks we get along fairly well. We usually just drink ourselves to sleep in front of the television. She makes coffee for me on Saturday mornings. Most Saturdays, we're drinking again by noon. On weekdays I sleep in a closet at the office building where I am the night custodian. Even though I've done it for over a year, I'm not too worried about being found out. Does anyone actually know the names of the people who clean their offices, their bathrooms, and their floors at night, let alone their comings and goings? Just to be safe, I work hard, chew lots of gum to cover my breath, and wash up in the mop sink.

This particular Friday I decided to hit a bar before I went over to the apartment. As often happens to me when I am in a bar, I lost track of time. A friend of mine walked in and slid in across the table of my booth.

"Anna is looking for you."

I looked at my watch. It was after ten.

"Oh crap," I said. "How do you know?"

"She sent her brothers out to find you. They were at my place."

That was not a good thing. She had two brothers and they were not nice people. They worked collections for an unsavory man. I never had any run-ins with them myself, but they had a certain dark edge about them that always made me uncomfortable when they were around. If she sent them out for me, that meant she was mad that I didn't show up with the booze. Even a quiet drunk can become a mean drunk when they don't have their elixir. Now that the liquor stores were closed, I had no way of toning down that anger.

I was afraid and I was inebriated to the extreme.

I didn't want to sleep outside and her brothers knew about my friend's house. The only place I could think to hide was my little closet at work. I didn't like to be there on weekends for fear the weekend crew would discover my living arrangements. However, I was out of choices. I slipped in the service entrance and made my way unseen to my little closet hideaway on the 6th floor. As I laid there on the make shift bed tucked behind a wall of shelving, I couldn't ignore the reality of my abysmal existence. It wasn't exactly my life plan to be a 55 year old drunk, living in a storage closet, penniless, and on the run from two thugs who wanted to give me a beat down for not bringing whiskey to their alcoholic sister. I seriously wanted to end it all.

It wasn't always this way. Only a few years ago, I had a wife and two lovely daughters. We lived in a nice home just outside a small town an hour or so from the city. I had my own construction business, which specialized in building churches and medical clinics. Then one day it all came crashing down on me, literally and figuratively.

During my oldest daughter's confirmation class they were discussing the Ten Commandments, specifically adultery. The pastor made an off-color remark to my daughter, Ginny, that she probably knew about the ill effects adultery can have on a family. (I had an affair once and that secret can't be kept in a small town.) Well, Ginny didn't know, and she was devastated by the pastor's insinuation. When she came home and told me about it I was out of control livid. The next morning I went straight to his office, walked right in and smashed him in the face, repeatedly. I told him if he ever embarrassed my daughter again I would end him. Only the shrieks of the secretary brought me up short. I stormed out the back door. As irony would have it, my company was actually putting an addition onto the church. On the way to my truck, one of my workers accidentally backed his Bobcat into a stack of bricks just as I was walking by. A skid broke loose and an avalanche of bricks knocked me down. The hand I had just used to pummel the pastor was crushed under the pile.

The charge was assault with intent to do bodily harm. I was sentenced to 18 months. I lost my company, my wife divorced me, and my arm was about 10% of what it was. My time in jail only caused my anger to seethe until it settled somewhere deep in me as a malignant, bitter, tumor. When I got out I didn't have any capital, my reputation was shot so starting a new company was out. Plus, no one in the construction industry was interested in an ex-con with one good arm. I finally found some work in the city as a custodian. With generous consumption of liquid anesthetic, my overwhelming bitterness gradually dissolved into one long drunken depression.

That night in a solvent smelling, 6'x8' prison cell of my own design, I did something I had never done in my entire life. I prayed.

"God if you're real, you know I have made a mess out of my life. I don't deserve your help. I'm probably beyond help. But I need help."

Then I went to sleep.

The next morning I got out of the building as soon as I woke up. I remembered an out of the way place on the other side of the city that was open early. A few minutes after my bus ride I was sitting at the far end of a long bar with dry toast and a Bloody Mary. I was the only patron until some young kid came in. Instead of following bar etiquette and sitting at the opposite end of the bar, he came and plopped himself down on the stool right next to me.

"Tough finding a place to sit?" I asked sarcastically.

"No."

"I'm not looking for company." I continued.

"Well," he hesitated a bit. "I believe I have been sent here to talk with you."

"Oh yeah. By who?"

"God."

71

The bartender started laughing. He was even older and crustier than me.

"I don't need a pamphlet or whatever else you're peddling." I snapped.

"I'm not selling anything," he replied calmly.

I was just about ready to tell him to get lost. Then I remembered my prayer from the night before and I had myself a pause.

"What do you want then?" I turned down my combative tone considerably.

"I know this is going to sound kind of weird. But, my wife and I were driving by here a little after 11:00 last night when I had a voice go off in my head telling me to come to this bar in the morning. I'm not saying I have some direct line to God or anything, but it was very clear and very strong. I pretty much ignored it. However, when I got up this morning I couldn't shake it. It was almost like a command and I found I was incapable of doing anything else this morning. So here I am."

I can't explain why, but I believed this kid's account and for some reason it terrified me and mystified me at the same time.

"What are you supposed to tell me?" I finally stammered.

Both our stools were now turned and we were knee to knee. He reached over and placed his hand on my bad arm. An unfamiliar warmth spread through my body when he touched me.

"God has totally and completely forgiven you." He said. "He wants you to know that and accept that."

I have never been so unprepared and at the same time so desperate to hear anything my entire life. I started visibly shaking. I was crying and I couldn't stop. My body was heaving and I crumpled into the arms of this kid. Then my bad arm started twitching. I sat up and flexed and clinched my hand.

"Look at my hand!" I yelled. I kept flexing it. I couldn't stop!

"What's so special about your hand?" the kid asked, oblivious to the miracle that had happened right before his eyes.

I told him the story.

The bartender listened too. He wasn't laughing any longer.

*　　*　　*

That all happened fourteen months ago. I have since dried out. A Christian man who owns a large construction company took a chance on me. I'm doing estimates and helping to manage crews. I have my own apartment and there is a Bible study group that meets there twice a month. I own a truck again. This very minute I am driving back to my hometown. My ex-wife agreed to meet me for coffee.

"For He will deliver the needy when he cries out for help, The afflicted also, and He who has no helper. He will have compassion on the poor and needy, And the lives of the needy He will save."
Psalm 72:12-13

Religion

I have come to detest religion. Although it wears a "from God" disguise, religion is man made, man inspired, and man centered. Generically it involves man creating a set of tenets and observances that are to be followed by the faithful. In its least destructive form, it may be a simple call to spiritual disciplines. It is at its most virulent and hurtful, however, when contemporary social mores are equated as "right" relationship with God. Abundant pressures for conformity accompany this type of religion. Just a casual read of church history should give us a chill and motivate us to avoid it at all costs.

There is a little episode that sheds some light on how we in the West practice our religion from time to time. The setting was the late 19th century in a moderate sized town in Ohio. A growing church hired a pastor from Indiana to come and pastor their flock. He came with his wife and four children. A fifth child was born soon after the move. Bishop Milton, (as he was known to his parishioners) soon became well respected for his sermons on hard work, personal resolve, and determination. He was a highly intelligent man and people often sought his counsel on a wide range of matters.

An emphasis on frugality was a major thread in the social fabric of the time. The Bishop himself was known to preach on it occasionally. However, a few people in the congregation felt he was a hypocrite on the issue. They claimed he was overly doting on his two youngest boys. They noticed he bought them, what was considered at the time, quite extravagant "toys." To make matters worse the boys soon tired of playing with the toys and would usually break them apart, sometimes resulting in the Bishop buying them more. The chatter in the congregation of the spoiling of these two young boys and the wasteful spending of the Bishop grew to the point where some members thought the matter should be brought to the church board for possible disciplinary action. After all, weren't the tithes and offerings of the members paying his salary? That money should be stewarded properly on food, shelter, clothing, and savings, not on frivolous toys for boys who abused them anyway.

For whatever reason and we don't know exactly why the crusaders never made it to the board and the momentum for such foolishness fizzled.

We can be thankful for that.

The Bishop was Bishop Milton Wright and his two young boys who took toys apart and reconstructed new and improved versions were named Orville and Wilbur.

"Who are you to judge the servant of another? To his own master he stands or falls; and stand he will, for the Lord is able to make him stand."

Romans 14:4

HELP

I worked the first and third Saturday morning of each month at
an odd, mostly unknown event called "The Little Pig" market. It was
where buyers and sellers of young piglets met in the back parking
lot of the county courthouse. I say odd because of the variety of
people involved and the uniqueness of the financial transactions.
The sellers came from remote rural locations. A seller could be
a pig farmer bringing one hundred forty little pigs in a trailer or a
family with a couple of pink squealers sitting in the back seat with
the kids. More than once I heard something like, "Bye Barney," as a
child bid farewell to his little traveling companion. The buyers were
generally large-scale pig farmers who bought the piglets and then
brought them to full market weight for sale to pork processors. The
sellers would park in a pre-arranged area while the buyers would
walk around and examine the goods. There was usually a bit of
bargaining, deals were sealed with just a handshake, followed by the
physical transfer of the pigs. The most excitement was when one of
the little rascals escaped. Watching four or five people chase a piglet
around a parking lot was high humor. My job was to record all the
transactions for the county record.

One of the buyers knew me. I had gone to school with his son.
He was well known in the county. Pigs were only a small part of
his operation. He had a beef contract with a fast food giant, two
sections of irrigated cropland, and he had six employees just to run
his turkey barns. I knew he graduated from the university and one
only needed to talk with him briefly to understand that he was an
expert in agribusiness. Even so, our exchanges were usually, "Hi.
How's fishing?"

One morning however, he actually started a real conversation
with me.

"Suppose you heard about Josh?"

Actually, I had heard. Off at college Josh had written some bad checks. Unfortunately for him one of them had been for an amount that pushed past the misdemeanor threshold. He used it to buy a motorcycle which he promptly crashed and he had no insurance. He was given six months in the county workhouse. It was not exactly the kind of educational experience his father had been paying tuition for.

"Yeah, I did. Sorry." I answered.

"Don't know what to do about that kid. Given him all he ever needed and he still thinks he needs more."

Given him all he ever needed was the truth. Josh had a new car the day after he passed his driving test. He had full use of his dad's 24-foot cruiser on the river, and he took at least a dozen ski trips every winter.

"Well, I cut him off," Mr. Hartwell continued. "Maybe he'll figure things out being on his own."

I mumbled something indistinct. This conversation was beyond my 19 years.

He continued anyway. "Farming is easy. Now parenting, that's another matter."

Many years have passed since the "little pig" market days. In that time I've been a parent, grandparent and in my profession I talk to parents on a regular basis. My experience has been that most of us are like Mr. Hartwell. We parent by instinct. We probably parent in a similar fashion as to how we were raised. He wasn't a bad parent. He wanted to provide the things for his children that he never had. Maybe the one thing he was trying to provide was not the thing Josh needed. Or maybe Josh was too immature to realize what was being provided for him.

How to parent? That is quite a question now isn't it? There are more than a few resources to choose from on the subject. A person could attend conferences by leading experts, reference countless video offerings, or read the latest best seller. Is there a pastor of a mega church in America who hasn't written a book on parenting?

There is so much information that you might feel failure is certain if you are not versed well enough. To be sure, the aids available offer valuable insights and strategies. But what if someone has not, or cannot avail themselves to all that is out there; or even a small portion of it? Is there something simple a sincere parent could remember in the midst of the busyness? Is there something significant and yet easy to focus on?

Maybe all our children need from us is a little HELP.

H: Hug and Hold
E: Encourage
L: Listen
P: Provide, Protect, Play, and Pray

There is empirical research that touts the benefits of hugging, holding, encouraging, listening, providing, protecting, and playing. The benefits of prayer are anecdotal. This is rather simplistic, yes. However, maybe if we take as many opportunities as we can to HELP our children, things might turn out fairly decent after all.

"Train up a child according to his way, Even when he is old he will not depart from it."

Proverbs 22:6

Harvest of Gold

The late October morning was crisp and the sky promised endless blue. The earliest rays of morning light penetrated the lower branches of the windbreak. There was no rustling of leaves on the crinkly stalks that had lost their summer green. They stood motionless to embrace the warming sun that would melt their frosty coat. A large doe carefully eased herself out to the edge of one row. Her reddish summer coat had given way to the gray shroud that allowed her to travel the winter woods as a silent ghost. Her left ear twitched. A drop of moisture fell from the black tip of her nose splashing on a partially frozen clump of soil. She was oblivious to the idea that she would be finding a new place to sleep tonight; a place without a ready-made morning menu. For today was the day each silent sentinel would yield its golden treasure.

On the other end of the field a man stood outside the pole barn that housed the great combine. He was slightly bent and his head was bowed. A few gray wisps peeked out under his wool cap. Wrinkles and age spots could not hide his strong chin or his clear, purposeful eyes. Although the skin on the back of his hands was almost translucent, they were still thick and immense, seasoned from decades of manual exertion. His walking was no longer a stride. He made his way around to the side of the John Deere with cautious steps. His overalls hung looser than they did earlier in his life, but his plaid lined, canvas jacket still looked like it had been tailor made.

"Thank you Lord," he whispered. "Thank you for your faithfulness and your kindness. You already know this is going to be the last time."

He slowly climbed the steel ladder leading up to the glassed in cockpit.

Minutes later the green behemoth was mowing down stalks and spewing dust into the sky. A torrent of golden kernels flowed from the top of the elevator into the trailing grain bins. By late afternoon the field was bare and the semi drivers were lashing down the tops of their overflowing trailers. The man stood in the open door of the barn. He stared out into the empty field and beyond. He stared back into time. His time.

At the peak of his career he farmed twelve hundred acres. When he retired, he starting selling off parcels. None of his children wanted to farm. He sold some to a neighbor, some to the DNR, and 160 acres to a housing developer. However, he kept a very special forty acres to himself. Many friends and neighbors speculated, but never understood why he kept this small piece of land and why year after year, without fail, he planted and harvested a crop. They knew he didn't need the money. When asked he'd simply say, "Like to keep my hand in it," or some other evasive response. They knew there was more but they never pressed him for it.

The elderly gentleman eased himself down on a backless wooden bench along the barn wall, letting the autumn sun warm him. He thought back in his time to sixty-three years earlier when he stood on these very same forty acres. They constituted a separate plot that was in addition to the original four hundred acre farm he was purchasing from his father's brother. He was a strapping twenty two year old with a new wife and a son on the way. He had bowed his head then also.

"Lord, I don't know how to be a father and I know I have a lot to learn about farming. But if you will teach me, if you will bless my family, I promise that I will give you the profit from everything that is grown on this field for as long as I live."

He closed his eyes and let his shoulders slide back into the wall. He folded his hands on his lap. His chin drooped into his chest and his breathing slowly subsided as he ever so quietly slipped away. His cancer finally reached the end of its course. A pair of chickadees perched on the top of the barn door, were the only earthly witnesses.

Four weeks later an anonymous cashiers check arrived at a local charity like it had every November.

"I shall pay my vows to the Lord,
Oh may it be in the presence of
all His people.
Precious in the sight of the Lord
Is the death of His godly ones."

Psalm 116:14-15

The Final Say

In our day it is difficult to escape the never-ending cacophony of opinions. Every television network has its own group of pundits with their well-rehearsed sound bites. Talk radio's surplus of vocal "visionaries" is deafening. Then there's the print media with the "professional" editorials, the syndicated "all stars," and public submissions from the experts. And now, with the Internet, we can blog, tweet, or podcast ourselves into an opinion labyrinth of dizzying proportions. It seems many are more than sufficiently obsessed with how we are to think, or not to think. We understand of course there are people with deep-rooted agendas trying to "sway public opinion." Whether it is a talk radio pontificator, a primped PBS smoothie, or the corporate owned anchors and editors, the battle for our minds, affections, and spending is extreme, escalating, and endless.

Escaping the deluge of debate is impossible without becoming a cloistered recluse. Many Christians respond to this situation by saying, "That's just the world. We're in it, but we're not of it."

Well, what about the church? Since the Judaizers first questioned Peter for speaking to the Gentiles, the church has been engaged in a two thousand year opinion Armageddon of its own. Our "holy war" has had its share and range of casualties. We've had beheadings and stake burnings. We have silenced scientists with the threat of death or imprisonment and excommunicated reflective writers. Our myriads of denominations are not historically rooted in peace and harmony. All of this has led to the less severe but no less troubling, quiet, apathetic, disconnected, massive retreat of the disheartened trying to distance themselves from the wrangling and somehow stay connected and relevant.

I'm guilty. I have not remained above the fray. I have been involved in my share of theological skirmishes. I've increased the volume and expanded the animation in proportion to the weakness of my argument. I've swung my orthodoxy around like a club, delusional in my thinking that knocking someone over with the "truth" will be of great benefit to them. Even sitting here writing about this, I'm not sure if I am lessening the mess or adding to it.

All of this causes me to reflect on the return of the Lord and the ceasing of all arguments. I remember my younger years when I looked forward to this event with the vain idea that my vindication would follow. Not only would Jesus end all opinion mongering, but obviously, my opinions would be the ones that would be victoriously upheld. After all, if my opinions were not right, I would not be holding to them.

I welcome the Lord's return now with a considerably different form of anticipation. I believe He will end all arguments but I no longer look for vindication. I simply hope God's grace will enable me to withstand my own humiliation. I look for an internal peace that will come with finally, fully, having the mind of Christ. I long for deliverance from the opinion war's virus of confusion, doubt, apathy, and cynicism. I relish the place of silence, all voices off . . . except His.

"For now we see in a mirror dimly, but then face to face; now I know in part, but then I will know fully just as I also have been fully known."

1 Corinthians 13:12

A Flicker of Light

Candace Weston started making bad "men" decisions at a young age. She had a daughter at fifteen, was married and divorced by twenty. At thirty, she was an unskilled single mother living hand to mouth. Over the years her daughter, Justine, had watched as her mother was used or abused by an inordinate amount of men. She remembered one year they had lived with three different men in three different places. Through it all Candace kept telling her, the "right guy" was going to come along. Justine considered her mother a desperate loser. She hated her for it and she hated herself for hating her mother.

Then came Mason Fieldman. Justine usually met her mom's "new guy" by surprise in the morning. They would either be in the bathroom or the kitchen. They were not always fully dressed, which was always an uncomfortable moment. Not so with Mason. He actually took them to dinner where the person who took your order was not standing behind a counter wearing a blue hat. He didn't use foul language. His clothes were clean and he was too. Most unusual, Mason didn't treat Justine like she was in the way. He talked to her, asked her questions, and actually listened to her responses. After some months, Justine actually reached a point where she hoped her mom and Mason would get together. Eventually, they did. Mason had his own house in a real neighborhood where you didn't see a gas station or a convenient store out the window. She went to a better school. She made a friend. She read an entire book.

After a few months the most slender glimmer of hope of a better future pushed its way into Justine's thoughts. Out of habit and heartbreak she knew she dare not nurture it. Any day now there would be a blow up. Her mom would scream or threaten and they would be out looking for an apartment again. She waited, but it didn't happen. All was calm. Her mom got a job working three days and one night shift a week at a hotel desk. Some days Justine forgot she hated her. Some days she almost felt she had a normal life.

The third time Candace's night shift fell on a Friday, Mason paid Justine a late night visit in her bedroom. He was drunk. It was not a welcome visit. At first she kicked and scratched and clawed, but he was too powerful. He inflicted pain until she submitted. When he was done he warned her not to tell or he would kick the both of them back out onto the street. He told her not to cry or he would come back and do it again.

She shmushed her face into her pillow to muffle her convulsing sobs.

Later, she heard him snoring. She crept down the hall. He was on the sofa. The television was on. His billfold and car keys were on the kitchen counter. She quietly packed a bag; stopping every few seconds to make sure Mason was still snoring. She tip toed to the kitchen and took the keys and billfold. Once outside she ran for the car.

She drove around aimlessly trying to form a plan. Eventually she parked on a side street downtown four blocks from the bus station. There was $45.00 and two credit cards in the wallet. And folded up in a semi-hidden compartment was a scrap of paper with Mason's ATM pass code. Justine left the keys in the ignition and the doors unlocked. An all night drug store had an ATM. She extracted all the money she could. At the station, she picked the most immediate departure with the farthest destination. Thirty-six hours later she stepped off a bus in San Antonio.

Alice Benson was the madam of a clandestine yet oft visited "massage parlor" and "escort service." If her girls stayed in line she treated them well with excellent living conditions, good pay, and a wide variety of agents for self-induced anesthesia. If they didn't, there was Wallace. He was a physical brute with a bestial brain. Alice had two clients who were willing to pay extreme dollars for a new face. This kept her ever on the look out. The bus station was one of her most productive recruiting haunts. She saw Justine coming miles away. Her skills at seduction were not limited exclusively to men. She and Justine were having lunch less than half an hour after Justine exited the bus.

"Need a place to stay?" was the lure. "See all the money," was the hook. Wallace was the gaff.

Girls don't spend much time dreaming they will grow up to be prostitutes. At nineteen, Justine (working name Crystal) was a three-year veteran. Every john was greeted with a smile that skillfully masked her contempt. Crystal liked money, but grew to curse every dollar she earned. Self-loathing and bitterness were constant companions. Alcohol and cocaine were her anesthetics of choice.

One afternoon her first "client" was Gabriel Mender. He was fifty-nine years old. Most of his hair had given in to grey. He carried twenty-five pounds more than was fashionable and he was shorter than he wanted to be. He had never visited a prostitute before. He'd known the existence of this brothel and had hemmed and hawed for some time about going. He finally reached a point where he could wait no longer.

On his way up the stairs he almost turned around to go back home. He was extremely nervous, yet his anticipation level was high.

Oh God, Crystal thought as she entered the room, *another old fart.*

Gabriel sat up in his chair a little straighter when she entered. He didn't realize she would be so young. Secretly he was glad. In Madam Benson's brothel you paid up front for allotments of time. He had bought a half an hour.

"Hi, my name is Crystal. Wallace tells me you're name is Gabe."

"That's right."

"What would you like to do this afternoon Gabe?"

"Would you mind just sitting down. I would just like to talk first."

If this guy's thing was talking, it was fine with her. She'd had talkers before. They were usually quick and easy.

"Crystal," Gabriel began. "What if I told you I know of a place where a young woman like yourself could go and be totally safe, a place where no man or woman wants to use you, a place where you would get to determine your own future and receive help doing so?"

Crystal did not answer. This was not the type of talking she was expecting.

"Please hear me out," he continued. "I know of such a place.

89

And I can get you there if you'd like."

Crystal had a couple of smart mouthed replies at the ready but she held her tongue.

"Would you be interested in such a place?"

She still didn't respond. She actually was a little startled and a bit confused.

"You didn't come here to get off? You won't get your money back you know."

Gabriel reached in his pocket and pulled out a card. One side of the card was black with The Portal embossed in white. The flip side was white with an address. Gabriel explained to her that The Portal was a haven for prostitutes and run away girls. It was started by a retired police officer who had copious financial backing from wealthy donors. The girls were taken to a different community if they wanted. They received housing, and counseling until they were independent. Some even went to school. They were able to forge new identities and a completely new life. It was all provided free of charge.

He held out the card for her.

She didn't take it and she was still suspicious.

"And just why would people do that?"

"They feel called."

"Called? What does that mean, called?" she almost spat out the words.

"They believe it's their service to God."

"Oh, so I suppose you think you are on a mission from God too?" She wasn't mocking him, but she was close.

Gabriel carefully weighed his thoughts before he spoke again. "Crystal, this is what I believe. Somewhere, sometime, some place, either you or someone who cares about you prayed to God. They prayed concerning you. God heard that prayer. Although His interaction with our personal timelines may make it seem like He doesn't hear. He does. And He set things in motion to answer that prayer."

Gabriel's mention of prayer sparked an explosion of memories for Crystal. Most of the memories were hurtful and scarring. But there was one memory that dissolved the others away. She remembered a small girl on a swing outside a house. Her mom was inside fighting with a man. The girl on the swing was afraid her mom would cry; afraid they would have to live in another place. The little girl turned her face to the sky. "God, are you real? I heard you were. Me and my mom need your help."

Somewhere in that hard to define place of mind, soul, spirit, and emotions, the tiniest little light of life flickered as Crystal replayed that day on the swing. With her angry, survival mode toughness, she tried to blow the flicker of light out.

It held fast.

She tried again. Fiercely.

It would not be extinguished.

Crystal sat down on the bed. She wondered if the man could tell she was shaking inside.

They both sat in silence.

After a few minutes she stood up and walked over to Gabriel. She leaned in and brought her lips close to the side of Gabriel's head.

"I'll need two cards." She whispered.

She put one card on the dresser and the other in a secret pocket in the waistband of her skirt.

Wallace was standing outside the door when Gabriel left.

"That was quick," he grumbled.

Crystal gave him one of the cards.

"He was trying to save me." She said mockingly.

Wallace examined the card. He chuckled and flipped it into a waste canister.

"He heals the broken hearted and binds up their wounds."

Psalm 147:3

Departure

What if? Really. What if the Lord parted the curtain, paid you a visit, and made the offer? Told you that you could leave with him that very minute. Would you be ecstatic or hesitant? Would you jump on board or would you not quite be ready for that yet. Would you even have a choice?

In my early teens, I read a short science fiction story about two young children, a brother and sister who, unknowingly, were playing near an opening to an inter-galactic wormhole. A friendly alien came through the passageway and invited the brother to travel with him back to his world. The description of the far away galaxy fascinated the boy. The alien spoke of unparalleled vistas and offered endless adventures. It was a world where a human would be free from the shackles of his mortal limitations and yet still retain his identity. However, there was a catch. The passage was going to be open for less than an hour and the brother's decision would be final. The wormhole would not open again in his lifetime.

I wish I could remember the name of the story and the author so I could reference both more respectfully. I'm not sure why, but I have thought of that story often over the course of my life. When I do, I think about my own departure. Although it may not be eminent, it is inevitable.

I am interested in delaying the inevitable as long as possible. If I were given the same option as Elijah and Enoch, I would have mixed emotions. I know theologically, in my head, it should be a no-brainer. No more cares, no more worries, pain free, all questions answered, new body, renewed mind, knowing the complete extent of His mercy and forgiveness, and seeing Him in the fullness of His majesty. But in my heart . . .

I want to see my grandchildren grow up, hugging and kissing them all along the way. I want to see my children reach their full stride in life. What about the well being of my wife? Although I'm pretty sure my bucket list will look foolish from across the divide, I still have some things I want to do and see. I've heard the lofty and soaring preaching from the first chapter of Philippians on how Paul desired to leave and explained that he was required to stay for the sake of others. The application being that if we truly had our minds set on the "things above" we'd feel likewise.

Well I don't. In fact I feel the opposite. The truth of my condition is that I desire to stay and hope I'm not required to leave. Unspiritual? Worldly?

I'm aware that eye has not seen, ear has not heard, nor has it even entered man's mind, all that God has prepared for those that love Him. I believe that. I am grateful for it. I look forward to its fullness. However, the real me is not "there" yet. It's still "here." Even though I have days where I say, "Take me now Lord." It is an expression uttered out of sheer frustration, not a declaration of devotion. The common human desire to live here, now, and for as long as possible, pulses unabated through my veins.

In the science fiction story, the brother leaves. He told his sister to explain everything to their parents and to tell them that he loved them. I wondered then as I wonder now. Was he selfish for leaving, or would it have been selfish for him to stay.

Possibly these thoughts border on intellectual foolishness; how many angels on the head of a pin type of thing. Or, possibly, they may cause us to consider why we are here in the first place and why we are here still.

"Enoch walked with God, and he was not, for God took him."

Genesis 5:24

Geopolitics, and
a Christian Girlfriend

The passion started for Tanner when he was eleven. His father, a well to do textile manufacturer took him to watch the 1972 Olympic Trials for swimming. Tanner was thrilled by the excitement of the spectators and the fierceness of the competition. When the winners on the podium received their medals, their pride and joy swelled in him as well. Although captivated by the meet, he was totally unprepared for the effect the men's 100-meter butterfly would have on him. The stirring of the crowd was noticeably more intense. When the starter said, "Take your mark," the entire pool complex was muted in electrifying silence. The loud starter beep sent the crowd into an unrestrained roar. Tanner had never seen the butterfly before but when he witnessed the explosive power and grace of the racers, the uniqueness of the stroke itself, and the effect on the crowd; the course for the next eight years of his life was set.

Tanner did not have the eye hand coordination one needed to excel in sports that involved a ball and none of his coaches ever expressed enthusiasm about his running ability. In the pool, however, he could explore his competitive drive to its fullest. In less than three years he held the national record for 14's and under. At 17 he had Division I offers from the top swimming schools in the nation. The endless hours in the pool, the strict diet, and the tireless pursuit of perfecting his stroke was paying off. When he signed his letter of intent his parents could not have been more proud.

Although the classroom at university was part of his life, his goal, his driving force, his all-consuming passion was to stand on the podium at the 1980 Moscow Olympics and receive the gold medal for the 100-meter butterfly.

In the spring of his sophomore year he was living large. He and his girlfriend, Julie, were enjoying one another on a regular basis, he had a new apartment, a great car, classes were going well, and he had just broken the national record at a swim meet in Indiana. The trials were around the corner. His vision was becoming a reality.

Combining goals with the determination and personal discipline to reach them is an honorable endeavor. And, when all signs point toward ultimate fruition, a person can live in the illusion that he is in control of his own destiny. Tanner's obsessive focus had left him unaware of certain events that had been swirling all around him; events that would shatter that illusion of control…and his dream.

In a dorm room on the other side of campus Julie had been meeting with a friend from one of her classes. They were studying the Bible. Patiently and with penetrating precision Julie's friend used the scriptures to point the way to Jesus. Julie was starting to see Him. One night she did.

Hundreds of miles away in Washington D.C., the President and some of his advisors were discussing the unthinkable, boycotting the Games. The cold war was so frigid it evidently numbed our leader's ability to think. What are the dreams and aspirations of a measly few thousand athletes when compared to the opportunity to lessen the luster on a political adversary's moment of global hospitality?

The crash came all in one day. First an argument with Julie. Becoming a Christian had changed her view of her own promiscuity. This did not sit well with Tanner. The conversation ended poorly. Less than an hour later the phone rang. It was a teammate on the swim team telling him to quick turn on the TV to see the president address the nation. The mastermind, foreign policy strategist told the nation he was not going to allow the U.S. Olympic team to attend the Moscow Games. Most of Western Europe followed suit.

At nineteen years old, the only adversity Tanner had ever faced was the timer's clock and the swimmer in the next lane; obstacles he had overcome with will power and training. He had no skills to cope with geopolitics and the affairs of the heart that were now disrupting his world. The overwhelming events of the day left his stomach churning and his head pounding. His unrestrained pacing just agitated him more. Finally, he went to the pool and swam and swam and swam until he couldn't lift his arms above the surface. When he finally stopped, he clung to the pool wall until his body started to chill, along with his heart, his mind, and his dreams.

Tanner's plunge into despair, swiftly turned terminal. He may have been a bit egocentric and immature, but he was practical. He chose the suicide method that would cost nothing and have no margin for error. He reasoned water would be fitting and the site was just a few blocks away.

At 2:00 am he was standing on the pedestrian hand railing of a bridge hundreds feet above the river. The clouds were low and saturated. Each streetlight was enveloped by a halo of vapor and watery reflections were visible everywhere. The slight mist that pressed against his face made all exposed surfaces slippery. Tanner held on to a light pole for balance. He scanned in all directions. He wanted to be sure there was not a soul in sight before climbing atop the railing. Convinced he was alone, he had determined he would go headfirst so his neck would break on impact. As he was contemplating how to keep his body in the dive position for the entire descent, a hand grabbed him from behind. Before he could resist, he was back on the bridge deck. He was in the vise grip of a black man well over six and a half feet tall. His massive hand completely encircled Tanner's bicep. The man did not speak. His trench coat was wet and water dripped off his wide brimmed hat. Tanner looked up at the strangers face. The man's eyes were piercing, penetrating, and yet they were kind all the same. They were knowing eyes and they seemed so very, very old. Tanner tried to shake free. The man's grip remained solid. The more Tanner resisted, the more the man's hand felt like a cast iron clamp.

Finally, Tanner broke. He melted into the giant stranger's arms. His chest heaved with each groan filled sob. After a few minutes, the crying stopped. The man picked Tanner up and carried him like a baby back to the apartment. He never asked for directions and Tanner didn't give any. He opened the door to the apartment without a key, still carrying Tanner in his arms. He walked straight to the bedroom and laid him on his bed. The stranger lifted his index finger to his lips.   He placed his other hand on Tanner's chest and held it there, firmly, until Tanner drifted off to sleep.

Tanner woke in the morning convinced he had been dreaming.

Puffy eyes, damp clothes, an unmistakable warm area on his chest, and an unexplainable peace dissolved those thoughts.

He picked up the phone.

"Julie? Hi. It's me. Can we talk about your Jesus thing? Something happened to me last night. I think you need to know about it."

"Are they (angels) not all ministering spirits, sent out to render service for the sake of those who will inherit salvation?"

Hebrews 1:14

The Widow's Penny

One of the unique aspects about the gospels are those times when we get to observe some of the private moments between Jesus and His disciples. The accounts of His teachings delivered to the general public, like feeding the five thousand, raising Lazarus, and clearing the moneychangers out of the temple, are all exceptional. Often, however, I find myself being drawn more and more to those small, intimate moments, where the Lord has something to say just for those who are standing at his side at the time.

Such is the case in Mark 12:41-44

And He sat down opposite the treasury and observed how people were putting money into the treasury; and many rich people were putting in large sums. A poor widow came and put in two small coins, which amount to a cent. Calling His disciples to Him He said, "Truly I say to you, this poor widow put in more than all the contributors to the treasury; for they all put in out of their surplus, but she, out of her poverty, put in all she had to live on."

There are some obvious lessons from this passage that we have all heard many times. God does not measure our giving on a gross receipts scale. He is interested more in our motives than our amount and of course no one is impressed with showy displays of charity.

What speaks to me about this widow is not that she gave all she had left, but rather, that she gave anything at all.

Have you ever gotten angry at church or at God and the way you demonstrated your displeasure was by closing up the checkbook? Maybe a thought has run through your mind similar to, "I'm not giving those people any of my money." Or, maybe during those times when the sky is closed, and God seems unreachable, and absolutely nothing is going your way, your response has been to clench your fist around your dollars.

Through the widow's mite we see that clinging to money out of disappointment or anger is like a spoiled child pouting and throwing a tantrum.

We don't know if the widow was old or young. All we know is her mate was gone and she was alone. Don't you wonder? Did she ever have words with God about that? Obviously, the members of her late husband's family did not, or could not redeem her, or provide for her as the law and their culture instructed. Did she ever have words with God about that? The religious system of the day, which evidently was receiving large sums from wealthy donors, was more interested in taking her two coins than meeting her needs (Or they wanted her house. See vs. 40). Did she ever have words with God about that? Compounding the family and institutional failure to provide, there weren't many options available for a widow in first century Palestine to earn an income. Maybe she had some words with God about that too.

What we do see is a woman with no means, no people, no support, and no knowledge of her next meal, placing an offering in the treasury of the house of God. She is exercising giving in its purest form, as an exceedingly personal transaction with God. Her two coins were insignificant to the temple officers. Did they even see them slip out of her hand? The beauty of it is that she was not giving her pennies to them any way. She was giving to God and her deposit was not insignificant to Him. According to Jesus, her giving won the day.

The treasury where this event happened had an interesting arrangement. There were seven bell-shaped openings emptying into seven chests. When a chest was full it would be carried away and replaced with a fresh one ready for more. These were placed on the colonnade surrounding the temple so a person could walk up and discretely (or pretentiously) deposit their offering. Often, as was happening this particular day, audiences gathered. There were the simply curious, those milling about talking with friends and neighbors, or those with scrutiny in their eyes and book keeping in their hearts.

When we read this passage we are compelled to ask ourselves,

"Do we see her?" A destitute woman, alone, walking across the city through busy streets and shadowed alleys, silently, with her two little coins in hand, up the stairs to the colonnade, standing in line behind a man with rings on his fingers, flowing robes, and a bejeweled turban. She is waiting for him to make his big noise as he drops his gold into the fluted channel and give a nod with a knowing smile to the treasury officer standing nearby. Do we see her quietly giving her coins back to God? Back to this same God who gives us money for worship but only gave her a pittance?

The widow's giving is an extreme act of faith. She has enough money for one last food purchase and yet, she gives it away. Is she telling God she knows He is her provision, not the coins in her hand?

I was always miffed at God when I read about Him requiring the first fruits of the harvests from the ancient children of Israel until one day I realized that when they gave the first fruits, it was their way of telling God that they believed He was going to provide more.

When I examine the periods of my life when my giving is sorely lacking, it is predominately because I don't believe I have enough to pay my bills and still give. It is when I don't see God as my provider or don't consider my income as a blessing. It is when I am under the illusion that I am doing the providing and my providing is not adequate enough for me to be generous. I am not rich after all.

Finally, giving transcends any ledger. It goes beyond supporting some cause, organization, or religious institution. There is a spirit to giving, a flow. It is only when we enter that flow that our giving becomes joyously unfettered. God measures our giving and/or our keeping, but not as a CPA. He measures our motives and attitudes. It is not possible to be a cheerful giver unless you can give by faith, as an act of worship, knowing that God is not examining how much, but rather, how come.

Where Do You Go to Church?

"This is where my family has always gone."

"I go there because it is the only (put denomination here) church in town."

"I love the music."

"I get a lot out of the preaching."

"They have excellent programs for my kids."

"They have the best nursery."

"It is only a few minutes from my house."

"Most of the members are businessmen like me."

"This is a beautiful building. I am proud to invite people here."

"They haven't wasted money on a building."

"I can serve there."

"They don't harp on doing stuff "for the church.""

"They meet on Saturday night."

"In and out in an hour."

"It is a beautiful long service that lasts most of the morning."

"My friends are there."

"I like what they are trying to accomplish."

"There is lots of excitement!"

"I love the free flow of the Spirit."

"The traditional liturgy means a lot to me."

"I like the written prayers."

"This is where God led us."

"We didn't like any of the other churches."

"It is the biggest church in town."

"I really like a small church where I know everybody. I like the feeling of family."

"I want to express my devotion with others."

"I like the anonymity."

"I like the pastor."

"The people are friendly."

"I can wear jeans."

"People dress up to show their respect."

"They don't ask for money."

And so it goes.

This is not an exhaustive list. It is however a list of what we have all heard people say over the years in regards to why they attend their particular congregation. In America especially, we know there are also racial, socio-economic, cultural, philosophical, and doctrinal motivations for particular church patronization. These reasons, more often than not, go unspoken. Yet their underpinnings are stalwart.

Somewhere in the course of church history the gathering together that was practiced by first century believers began to organize, which led to formalize, evolving into institutionalize. Then these institutions began to strategize, globalize, politicize, and finally, franchise. I am not bemoaning these developments or defending them. I am not offering a way to change them or advocating that they should be. However, for the last few centuries Christians all over the world do something that is universally called "going" to church. And of course, we choose where we go to church for as many reasons as there are churches to "go to". Maybe contemplating the reasons of others might help us examine our own. By doing so, maybe, we might find out what "church" is. And maybe we can rest in the idea that God did not lay out a blue print.

"Let us consider how to stimulate one another to love and good deeds, not forsaking our assembling together as is the habit of some, but encouraging one another; and all the more as we see the day drawing near."

Hebrews 10:25

104

Westbridge

When the application came in the mail I wasn't sure I should even fill it out. I had heard there were over 200 applicants for every opening they had. My letters of recommendation were solid but my GPA wasn't anything to tell your friends about. Someone "in the know" informed me that in order to get the applications down to a manageable number, the first cut was simply by GPA. I didn't know anyone who could put in a good word for me and I figured they would probably hire from within anyway. The application itself was daunting; five pages of questions ending with an essay section on why you should be considered for employment. Feeling all was hopeless, I was about to toss it when my wife reminded me that I had nothing to lose but the time needed to fill it out.

So I did.

However, the spaces on the application to answer questions were small and the instructions were implicit to only use the space provided. (It was the 80's. Electronic applications hadn't arrived on the employment scene yet.) Mistakes were a sure thing and I didn't relish the prospect of trying to white out ink, so I used a pencil. I wrote as neatly as I could and sent it off. I don't remember exactly what I said on the essay portion but I am sure it was as eloquent as blah, blah, blah can be.

Then my wife and I went on a planned extended vacation, overseas at that.

When we returned I had an urgent message to get a hold of Gary my former employer. The job I no longer had was a temporary position filling in for someone on a leave of absence. She was coming back and they had no other openings. However, Gary appreciated the work I had done for them and was active in helping me secure another opportunity.

"The people over at Westbridge want to talk to you. You need to contact them and set up an interview."

So I did.

My appointment was for 1:00 pm. I made sure I was there 10 minutes early. When I walked through the main door only a third of the hallway lights were on. Most of the work areas were dark and no one was seated in the main office. My first thought was that I had come to the wrong building. I wasn't sure where I should wait or if I should wait. My watch told me I had better make up my mind pretty soon. At the peak of my indecision I saw someone coming down the hall to my right. He was slender, almost gaunt, a couple of inches shorter than me, and his hair was pepper gray.

"Too old to still be working," I thought.

He was wearing dark blue pants and a light blue shirt with the company logo on the pocket. Above the pocket "Bill" was embroidered in heavy red thread. A crescent wrench handle was sticking out of one back pocket and a rag out of the other.

"Everyone is out to lunch. You must be the new guy they are hiring in product development."

He greeted me warmly and held out his hand. They were hands that had worked in oil and grease and dirt and dust for years. Honest hands.

I shook it gladly.

"I haven't been hired as of yet," I replied. "I haven't even had an interview."

"I can tell you the job will be yours if you want it. John (the boss) isn't bringing in anyone else to interview unless you turn it down."

I thought this was getting weird. How would a custodian know the employment decisions of the head of the company?

"You know," he continued. "Sometimes he doesn't have anyone to talk to. So he talks to me once in a while. I know a great deal of what goes on around here."

"Sounds encouraging," I replied still a bit suspicious of the quality of his information.

"You should wait for him in his office."

There was no way I wanted to wait in his office before he was even there.

"I don't think that's such a good idea. I'll just wait in the reception area."

"Ok. But you should at least have a look inside. The door's open. C'mon."

So I did.

The office was modest. A small round table with four cloth upholstered office chairs was squeezed in one corner. Two straight back leather chairs faced the desk. But it was what filled the entire wall behind the desk that brought me to a halt. It was a gigantic bronze bust, a relief of Christ from the shoulders up. It was stunning. How someone could create a warm facial expression, a penetrating gaze, and flowing hair out of metal was a mystery to me. Underneath the artwork John 3:16 was etched on frosted glass.

When I was done surveying the room, I looked over at Bill. His eyes were smiling.

"I better get back to work." he said. "Good luck."

I sat in the outer office and waited for my interview.

When John did arrive he was amiable. He shook my hand firmly and told me he was glad to finally meet me. The interview was nothing like what I was expecting. It was more of him showing me around the building, explaining what went on at different locations, and explaining how he saw me fitting in to their plans. He even showed me where the private coffee stash was, the good stuff. At the end of the tour we sat in his office and had an informal chat. We talked about business philosophy, where I saw myself in ten years, family, and even hobbies. He then told me something that made me chuckle.

"I see you filled out your application in pencil."

"Yeah. I saw the space limitation and didn't want to use white out."

"You know NASA spent thousands of dollars developing a pen that would work in zero gravity. The Russians used pencils." He grinned.

107

The contract offer was fair and he wanted me to sign.

So I did.

As I was pulling out of the parking lot I caught sight of Bill working on an outside water faucet. He turned and saw me. He flashed a big grin and waved so long.

My second day on the job during one of my breaks, I wandered about trying to find Bill. I wanted to say hello and thank him for his encouragement on the day of my interview. I also wanted to really find out why he was so confident I would be offered the job. He was nowhere to be found. Must be on vacation I surmised. When I still hadn't seen him after a week I went in to talk to John.

"Where's Bill?"

"Bill who?"

"You know, Bill the custodian. I never caught his last name. He is an older guy, slender, gray hair, wears frameless glasses. He told me you talk business with him occasionally."

John adjusted his seat and sat up a bit straighter. His expression was more than quizzical.

"The only custodians we have here are Tony, Ray, and Lisa. They're all younger than me. I can't say I actually talk business with them."

"But I met Bill on the day of my interview. He was working here. He had the uniform, company logo and everything. He told me everyone was out having lunch and that was why the building was dark when I arrived. He even told me the job was mine for the taking and that you weren't planning on interviewing any one else unless I turned the job down."

John's eyes widened. Like eyes do when a person is experiencing that mixture of mystery and fear. I could tell he was thinking. His mind was searching. I was half expecting him to scratch his head any moment.

"I thought those thoughts," he finally whispered. "But I never spoke them to anybody."

We let that thought hang about for a few seconds and then as if we had received a cue from a movie director we simultaneously looked at the huge Jesus on the wall.

And then at each other.

I am not sure if it stemmed from reverence, confusion, or what, exactly, but neither one of us spoke about Bill again.

"The mind of man plans his ways, but the Lord directs his steps."

Proverbs 16:9

Truth

One difficulty reading the Bible is that you don't get to hear the speaker's inflection. You aren't able to see facial expressions, eye movements, or body language. One of the places I've found this shortcoming most profound is Pilate's interview of Jesus. It is a passage where I wish the Bible were a high definition DVD filmed from three angles with crisp digital sound. Instead, we are left with our imagination to establish the sights and sounds, the interplay between the characters, and the reactions of the bystanders. A few years ago a famous Hollywood film star produced an elaborate film on Passion of the Christ. When I went, this was the one scene I bought my ticket to see. I was interested to find out if the scholars he had hired to help him with the script, interpreted Pilate's reaction to Jesus the same way I have.

They did!

After Jesus tells Pilate that He has come to bear witness to the truth, Pilate disdainfully spits out, "What is truth?"

I've never thought he asked the question jokingly. I didn't believe he was asking out of inquisitiveness, expecting a lesson from the teacher either. Rather, I always thought his question was actually a statement spewing forth from the core of his cynicism. Truth? There's no such thing as truth. Only weak-minded and imbeciles cling to the idea of truth.

Today, we as believers have to navigate through the same cultural milieu that Pilate did in his time. We live in a world where the most tolerated and respected views are the ones that make no claims of truth. In fact, any claims of truth are not only not tolerated they are scorned. All is relative. Everyone has his or her own truth. University professors throughout the western world earn tenure by demonstrating there is no truth; all the while being quite confident in the truth of that proposition.

We have a challenge. If we do actually know a truth or part of the truth and are compelled to share it with others, how do we not come off as know it alls or infallible zealots? If we are to effectively engage others to consider the truth of Jesus, we must recognize that the people we desire to become aware of God's love for them have been living in a life long environment saturated with the belief there is no such thing as truth in the first place.

So, how do we share the truth in love?

Maybe we should try it with very few words.

"Therefore Pilate said to Him, 'So you are a king?' Jesus answered, 'You say correctly that I am a king. For this I have been born, and for this I have come into the world, to testify to the truth. Everyone who is of the truth hears my voice.' Pilate said to Him, 'What is truth?' "
John 18:37-38a

For the Birds

Reeds at water's edge
Gently tousled by warm breezes.
High summer sun
Replaces spring green
With burnt tips of brown and tan.
Ancient white pines, black trunks, majestic bows
Soar skyward
Casting shadows of cover
The solitary hunter wades
Stick like, silent, at shadow's rim.
Gray blue coat, motionless
Black crowned spear, poised
Yellow eyes, alert
Scanning with rhythm of air and water
Pause, focus, aim
Thrust!
Eye blink speed
Spear held high
Silver green trophy clamped
Thrashing ceases
Disappearing down the great spear's shaft.
Pterodactyl wings lift
Gliding off to hidden shores.

At our summer place, my wife and I enjoy watching birds in all aspects of their behavior, especially their tireless quest for food. This has given me pause to think on the Lord's comments during the Sermon on the Mount about how birds are fed.

"Look at the birds of the air, they do not sow, neither do they reap, nor gather into barns, and yet your Heavenly Father feeds

them. Are you not worth much more than they?"

Matthew 6:26

In context, Jesus is addressing the tension that exists around serving God or serving money. He is speaking to the a common worry that creeps in on all of us, "Will we make it?" It is a practical issue that transcends time, cultures, and geography. Jesus is correct. Birds don't plant, harvest, or store. They do work however.

We have a number of great blue herons (See poem above). They stalk sunfish and small bass in front of our cabin. Their routine is one of daily vigilance and precision. Eagles and ospreys are constantly soaring above the lake scanning for fish. Not every dive bomb provides a catch. They will not stop until a meal is secured. Bluebirds, swallows, and martins fill the air of dawn and dusk gulping mosquitoes and flies. Woodpeckers tirelessly tour the woods with their herky-jerky hop, hunting down ants and unsuspecting dragonflies. Robins dutifully patrol the yard digging for juicy worms. Geese and ducks are bottoms up as they harvest bugs, plants, and crustaceans under water. Sand hill cranes work the fields with their long graceful strides. Loons are fishing all the time. They dip their head below the surface to have a look and then streak after their prey. Hummingbirds buzz from flower to flower to flower for nectar trying to sate their unquenchable appetite. Then there is the persistent hunting of hawks and owls. No one drops carrion at the doorstep of the turkey vultures either. They circle many miles on their scouting sorties. Crows…well every species needs a garbage clean up crew.

I love the implication of the names of some of our birds: flycatcher, gnatcatcher, grouse, nuthatch, grosbeak, roadrunner, creepers, thrashers, woodpeckers, turnstones, swallows, dippers, and of course the kingfisher.

I also marvel at some of the unique features birds have been gifted with. A hummingbird can remain stationary and fly backward, a handy skill when you get your food by probing a flower. The osprey has unparalleled eyesight and their eyes can work independently of each other. Loons swim faster than fish. An owl is soundless in flight. A pileated woodpecker can open a hole in a dead tree the size of a baseball in less than a minute. Herons can become a branch or a willowy reed as they patrol the shallows. Robins can actually turn their heads and hear movement just below the ground's surface. My favorites are cedar waxwings. They share. They will pass berries from bird to bird while sitting in a row along a branch of a green mountain ash.

When the Lord said, "Your Heavenly Father feeds them," I don't think He was thinking of the way commercially grown poultry are fed. He wasn't advocating sitting around clucking, waiting for the grain wagon to pull into the yard. I'm not hearing "sit back, relax, don't worry, be happy, God will take care of everything." I believe, I am safe in inferring that we too have gifts and abilities that He has given us. If, like birds we develop them with industry, and employ them with skill and service, God's provision will follow. We are not to be anxious or worry about that provision. But rather, focus on the character of God. He does tell us we are of great value to Him.

Birds teach us one more valuable lesson. In verse 25 of Matthew 6 Jesus asks, "Isn't life more than food?" Even though birds are diligent in procuring their daily bread, they soar, they play, they build, ... and they sing.

Crossing the Line

Brenda Larson was nervous as she directed her shiny black Lexus into the parking lot of the crisis pregnancy center. The only available space was between a dull blue Dodge Caravan and a green two door with a gray quarter panel on the front driver's side. She glanced one more time at the business card she had been holding in her hand all morning. She felt out of place.

Up until today her life had followed a course of extreme premeditation. For years she followed her plan meticulously. She went to the finest Christian college with hunting in her blood and a MRS. degree in her sights. She poached her man before the end of her sophomore year. He was a finance major destined to become a major player in the banking world. Their three children attended the most exclusive prep school in the city. Their home was featured in a prestigious architectural magazine. Friends were hand-selected for their potential future usefulness or for their social status. She sang in the choir at a church that boasted a three thousand seat auditorium, marble tiled restrooms, and a million dollar multi media system. She supported a number of causes with small tokens from her checkbook and she always voted for the morally upright political candidate. She strained tirelessly to retain complete control over her life (and the lives of those who orbited around her). She had been the puppet master of all this for years, quite successfully, until yesterday.

Her women's group at church met once a month. They always hosted entertaining speakers ranging from an executive of a leading Christian women's magazine to a horticulturist who had her own gardening show on television. Yesterday however, the speaker was a woman who waded in quite a dissimilar stream. Her name was Sylvia Prentiss. She ran a pregnancy counseling center in the inner city. She was a decade older than Brenda. Her clothes were plain, her make up was rather Spartan, and her graying hair was straight and simple. First impressions had Brenda bracing herself for an unpleasant and unpolished presentation. She wasn't all that enthralled about the topic either. Brenda believed only stupid or loose girls got themselves pregnant. They made their bed, so to speak. They could lie in it. That all changed when Sylvia began talking. It was obvious from the start that her intelligence was formidable. She had her bachelor's degree at twenty and passed the bar at twenty-three. Yet, it was her stories and her passion that held the women transfixed.

"I don't mean to be overly blunt," she said in closing. "But some of you ladies here in this room have gone great lengths to surround yourself in your own carefully constructed cocoon. You have an awareness that life exists outside that cocoon, yet you have never been face to face with someone from that world. You have never held a broken and troubled heart in your hand."

These last words of Sylvia's were a bomb. Somehow they bypassed Brenda's brain and penetrated directly to some deeper place. Sylvia's closing remarks didn't convict Brenda. They didn't make her feel guilty. They didn't cause her to emote. They didn't even propel her to take up a cause. Nonetheless, they performed a work. Some might argue a miraculous work. Those words changed her. And she knew it.

It was not, "Oh I need to change," but rather "Oh, I just changed."

After the talk was over, Brenda waited for Sylvia in the foyer.

"Could I speak with you for a moment?"

Sylvia stopped and smiled. "Of course."

"I think I want to come out of my cocoon?"

Sylvia was a no nonsense kind of person. She handed Brenda a card. "Meet me here tomorrow morning at 9:00."

Tomorrow morning had arrived. Brenda tucked the card in her purse. Despite her apprehension, she entered the building. There was a reception counter that separated the modest lobby from a hallway leading back to Sylvia's office and two other private rooms.

A small sign next to the receptionist's computer read, "First names are fine."

She was ok with that.

"Hello, my name is Brenda. I'm here to see Sylvia."

"Are you from the church group she spoke at yesterday?"

"Why yes I am." Brenda brightened a bit.

"She's the second door on the left and you can go right in."

The door was open. Someone else was already in the room with Sylvia. It was a young girl. She'd been crying.

"Am I interrupting?" Brenda asked tentatively.

"No, no," Sylvia assured her. "Please come in."

Besides a desk and a swivel chair positioned by the window, the only furniture in Sylvia's office was a high back upholstered chair and a sofa. Sylvia was sitting in the chair. Brenda was forced to take the remaining sofa space next to the young girl.

Sylvia made the introductions.

"Audrey, this is Brenda. Brenda this is Audrey."

Brenda smiled and recited her best, "Pleased to meet you."

Audrey mumbled a rather subdued, "Hello."

"Brenda," Sylvia began. "Audrey's pregnancy test came back positive and she is here to discuss her options with us. I have already told her you might be joining us and she agreed that would be ok."

Brenda thought to herself, "I didn't know I'd be joining this. I thought I was just coming to talk to you." But then she remembered she did ask about coming out of the cocoon.

Sylvia turned toward Audrey. "Audrey you know we are here to help you. Do not be embarrassed or ashamed. You are safe here. You can talk to us."

Audrey's beauty although unsophisticated, was stunning. She had thick natural brownish blonde hair. Her face was fresh with a perfect complexion highlighted by an ever so slight smattering of freckles. She had large brown eyes that were sharp and clear and still retained a measure of innocence. She was wearing jeans and a nice sweater. Her only jewelry was a single stranded silver bracelet.

She was sixteen, but a casual observer wouldn't have been able tell if she was fourteen or twenty. Her mother died when she was ten. Her father was ill equipped and not particularly disposed to raising a daughter by himself.

"It happened so fast. I wasn't prepared for it." She began. "I had only been out with this boy a few times. One night we started kissing and one thing led to another and I didn't know how to stop. After that night we couldn't stay away from each other." Her speech was frequently interrupted with little sobs and sneezes.

Sylvia handed her some more Kleenex.

"Now he doesn't want to have anything to do with me or a baby," she continued, her words coming faster and faster. "He says he'll help pay for an abortion. My dad is angry. He said he's not going to have a pregnant daughter parading around his house. I don't want to have an abortion. I just know I can't kill a baby. But, I'm not ready to be a mom. I don't know what to do."

Audrey started sobbing again, in earnest.

As Brenda was listening, she started wrestling with some powerful images. They were almost vision like. She saw the spare bedroom with its own private bath in the lower level of her house. She saw the enormous balance in her checkbook, which at the moment seemed strangely obscene. She saw the face of her neighbor Michelle, the gynecologist. She saw Audrey in her kitchen on a sunny morning drinking orange juice. Brenda's husband was in the kitchen too, drinking coffee and smiling. She saw the faces of a childless young couple taking the baby home from the hospital in a blue blanket. The scenes were all beautiful, yet unsettling. Their intensity was far outside any of Brenda's previous experiences.

She then sensed the Holy Spirit draw a line in the sand: stay on her side of the line, in her carefully crafted, neat as a pin world, or cross over the line into another way of doing life.

Then another wholly new sensation came over Brenda. Her stiff, calculating heart melted. She felt a love for Audrey. A real love, not some self-serving warm emotion. She reached over and gently placed her hand on Audrey's forearm.

Audrey wiped her face and eyes. She raised her face and finally her gaze toward Brenda.

"If you would be willing, you can come and live in my home. We have extra space. I'll walk beside this with you to the end. I'll be with you as much as you want me to be. I don't want you to worry about doctors or expenses either."

"But I don't . . . why?" Audrey was verbally stumbling, not fully being able to comprehend the offer.

"Because I can and I want to."

Sylvia leaned back in her chair as Audrey and Brenda hugged each other, tears flowing, lives melding.

"...And who is my neighbor?"
Luke 10:29

Genie in a Bottle

Our pastor was admonishing the congregation a few Sundays ago. He mentioned that some of us wanted God to be like a genie emerging from a bottle in a puff of smoke to grant us wishes. He suggested that for some Christians, prayer wasn't much different than rubbing the side of the lamp. In fairness to the pastor, these comments were offered up in the context of encouraging us to get beyond ourselves and stretch out our prayer life to encompass others.

As often happens to me while sitting in church, my thoughts strayed off on a path somewhat divergent from the one the pastor was trying to lead me down. I couldn't quite get that picture of God as a genie out of my mind. For some weeks afterward I imagined a number of scenarios where I stood before the Father and He would ask me if I could be granted three things and three things only, what would they be? A wish for more wishes was never an option.

I fantasized over a wide variety of choices: power to heal people and cure diseases, ability to time travel, wealth accumulation, mind reading, physical abilities like superman... and the list just got goofier.

However, when I seriously contemplated what I would ask for, if I really only could have three things granted to me, the choices became obvious. I would choose to receive the forgiveness of God, the mercy of God, and the grace of God.

"If you ask Me anything in My name
I will do it."

John 14:14

123

Legacy

My hometown in north central Minnesota is small enough that when there's a death, friends and neighbors show their love with food. The afternoon before my mom's funeral while the rest of the family was at the church making arrangements I was manning the back door as a long stream of casseroles, cakes, breads, fruit baskets, meat/cheese platters, and homemade bars made their way to my parent's house.

Accompanying every food offering were words of kindness and affection. Some would stop in for coffee; others didn't feel comfortable enough to intrude. Beth Hempstead delivered a pound cake. I vaguely remember meeting her once as a child. Her husband worked in the same place my dad did and somehow I knew she was from my mom's hometown.

"Jeff, I was wondering if I could tell you a story about your grandfather?"

My grandfather? That seemed odd. I'd never met my grandfather. He died when my mom was fifteen. I knew he was a doctor and that he had been a surgeon in a field hospital at the Battle of the Bulge. The only picture I'd ever seen of him was wearing his army helmet and chomping on the remains of a fat cigar.

"Ok? Sure. Come on in," I replied.

We sat at the drop leaf table edged against a far wall in the kitchen.

"How much do you know about your grandfather?" she began.

"Not too much. I wished I had talked to mom more about him."

"Well I think you might appreciate this."

"Please." I offered, extending my hand her way.

"This took place in late February of 1937. At that time he was a small town doctor, in fact the only one in town. A horrible blizzard had swept in. Heavy wet snow with horrific winds. You could hear the snow pelting the sides of your house. Many a tree folded under the weight. It started in the early evening and was still howling the next morning. That was when your grandpa got a phone call from Frank Berning.

"He was in a panic. His wife was in labor and things were not going well.

"People didn't have four-wheel drives back then. This snow was too deep anyway. Your grandpa called Wally Gerber who owned a big tow truck. He figured it was the only vehicle in town that had a chance. Within minutes they were making their way out to Berning's farm four miles from the north end of town.

"The snow was blinding.

"They weren't always sure they were on the road. With over a mile to go they swerved off and got stuck. The more Wally tried to get out, the deeper the truck sank.

"So they headed out on foot. Wally was a big strapping young man. He led the way. Your grandpa followed dragging his medical bag behind him.

"They were barely able to see from telephone pole to telephone pole. When they couldn't, they used the wire above their heads as a guide. They sank past their knees and fell down many times. Snow pelted their faces and the cold was starting to numb them both. Every step took extreme concentration and physical exertion. Just when they were starting to think it might be over for them, they spotted the yard lamp next to Berning's barn.

"There was a rope attached to the pole. Many farmers in those days had taut ropes stretched from house to barn in the winters because of blowing snow. When they got to the porch they had to use their hands to dig away enough snow to get the porch door open.

"Mae Berning was in a bad way when they entered the room. Her hair was wet and stringy and matted down. She was in mid scream as an unusually painful contraction swept through her.

"Then your grandfather took over. He had just seen Mae a week earlier in his office. All her babies had been over nine pounds and this one was breach. He knew attempting a normal delivery would be extremely risky for her.

"Frank, get a compress for her head. Wally, get two pots of water boiling."

"While those two were busy he leaned in close to Mae.

"I'm going to have to take this baby by surgery Mae. I'm going to give you a shot. When you wake up, you'll be holding the little one in your arms."

"She squeezed his hand with her approval.

"He did the actual surgery on the dining room table. They turned on all the lights and brought lamps in from other rooms. Miraculously there were no complications and the baby gave out a healthy cry when he swatted her on the behind. Your grandfather was extremely meticulous in sewing Mae back together.

" 'Going to do this right,' " he said.

"It was two days before they were dug out and roads became passable. Your grandfather received a box of bacon, some chickens, and two large hams as payment for his house call."

Abruptly, the story ended. She tilted her head down, lifted her eyes toward me, and her lips turned upward ever so slightly in a wry little smile. There was a soft quietness in the kitchen. It was heavy and it enveloped us both in a magical suspension. The story was a special gift and it warmed me. Yet, I was hoping there was more. We sipped our coffees.

"Thank you for that," I said. "I didn't know that story."

"My pleasure. Telling you was the first thing I thought of when I heard about your mom."

"There is one thing I don't quite understand," I continued. "How do you know so much detail?"

"Beth is a nickname. My given name is Elizabeth. I was named after your grandmother. I am the little girl born in that farmhouse that day."

"A good man leaves an inheritance to his children's children."

Proverbs 13:22

Forgive and Forget

God offers forgiveness. The fullness of the forgiveness and the free nature of His offer is one of the defining realities that separates the gospel from the foundations of all other philosophies or faiths. We receive by asking and benefit by receiving. There are no strings attached or prerequisites required. God's offer of forgiveness reveals His character, His purposes, and that He is by very nature, not human.

Of course, there is more to the forgiveness story. Jesus expanded the implications of forgiveness beyond God's offer toward us. He taught at length about our need for an active forgiveness permeating our day-to-day lives. He worked out a little math problem with Peter, detailing how our forgiveness of others, is to have no limits. He then discloses the personal tragedy and loss that is possible if we cannot forgive as we have been forgiven. In another setting His feet are being washed with the hair and tears of a street woman. This is happening in the home of a Pharisee who has taken offense at the display of devotion. The Lord reveals to the man of religion that we only love much when we realize we have been forgiven much. The implication being that if we are persuaded we have little or nothing to be forgiven for, we will love and forgive little. Jesus then raises the bar heavenward by teaching that if we really want to be like God, we shall love our enemies and forgive those who painfully mistreat us. That teaching looms over me as an enormous impossibility.

I understand all this. I recognize the source of power to forgive comes only from God and that some acts of forgiveness are truly supernatural. I know I place shackles on myself when I don't forgive. I grasp the truth that to enter into forgiveness is to enter into godliness. This leads to me to a personal dilemma.

There is one person I have had an extremely hard time

forgiving. I just can't seem to let him off the hook. He has done and said things that are inexcusable. A couple times his naiveté, lack of alertness, lack of involvement, and lack of love caused life long hardship for others. I try to forgive him. However, when I replay in my mind some of these specific breakdowns in integrity and character, when I remember some of his callous and selfish behavior, my anger and my inability to forgive rise to the forefront. I know God has forgiven this person. That helps, but it hasn't been enough. I have heard all the messages on the topic. I've been fed all the clichés. It is not that I refuse to forgive this person. I just don't know how. I have tried and tried and still try. When I think I have forgiven all and have put it to rest, a memory will become fresh and forgiveness is swallowed up by tension once again.

The person, who I cannot seem to forgive, is me.

Oh to be like God who not only can forgive, but can forget.

"Brethren, I do not regard myself as having laid hold of it yet; but one thing I do: forgetting what lies behind and reaching forward to what lies ahead, I press on..."

Philippians 3:13

Morning Coffee

It is an early morning Sunday and pleasantly warm. I am on the patio sipping coffee loaded with my favorite heavy cream. The canopy of an ancient maple spreads out majestically overhead while Mr. and Mrs. Cardinal are picking out sunflower seeds at the feeder and a chipmunk is busying himself with buried treasure under the hostas. Lilacs are blooming. Their lavender scent flavors the spring air. A giant dragonfly takes a time out on my knee, resting from his most recent mosquito patrol. Various disconnected thoughts amble into my consciousness and with as little mental exertion as possible, I lazily consider or dismiss them, one by one.

My coffee is still hot. Simple pleasures and all is well.

My solitary repose is shattered by a booming voice. It is too clear to be amplified, too loud to be human. Sound waves rattle the windows and sway the branches. I run out into the yard to have a better look. The entire sky is filled with flying horses. I spin and scan in all directions. Pegasus everywhere. They are white with flowing manes, their bridles are gleaming gold, and atop each one sits an angel. They don't look exactly like the depictions of angels I've seen before. But there is no doubt. Their hair is silver and their eyes are penetrating. Their skin is a multi shaded flickering bronze and they are bigger than life. They are hovering, waiting and when they turn just right I can almost see through them.

Then an outrageously loud trumpet blast rocks me out of my stupefied condition. Every head turns.

The One is coming.

He is mounted on an even greater horse. His robe is red stained and dripping. He has a great turban on his head. It is studded with glistening jewels of many colors. His name is

131

embroidered on His sash and He has a horrible sword belted to His side. All the angel's heads are bowed as He passes by while their horses whinny and stomp their approval.

He stops.

All of earth and heaven are still. He waves His hand and the angelic mounts swoop down from the sky. Thousands upon thousands of them streak toward the earth. One of them heads straight for me. He reaches out and grabs my up stretched arm and swings me onto his mount.

I don't even spill any coffee.

Up, up, up I go. There are many friends from church riding horseback with angels too. There are other friends and family and people I haven't seen for years. We're all waving at each other. Everyone has smiles on their faces so big that they couldn't wipe them off if they tried. As I soar higher I see people from all over the world being taken up and I am in awe.

I am not sure what to do with my coffee.

Tears of joy stream down my face and I feel emotions of ecstasy that I didn't know were possible. Then I start to see people who died years ago. I recognize them and am thrilled to see them. I finally notice that they look different than the last time I saw them. They have fantastic bodies that are fit and healthy. But they have a glow about them that makes it look like they're not merely physical. I turn to look at Jesus and I see a twinkle in His eye. Then I feel a great dark heavy weight leave me. I look at myself and I have a new heavenly body too! The life long war that raged inside me between the old man and the new man is over. The old man is not just metaphorically gone. He's gone!

I wish I'd left my coffee on the patio table.

Then I marvel at the Lord.

He is surrounded by all the saints of all time. Millions of millions are marveling at Him. Even though I believed, I had my doubts. Now all those doubts are gone. Hope is fulfilled. It is so exciting and fantastic I can't believe it. But, I don't have to believe any more because I am seeing it. I'm feeling it. I'm living it! I look around. There are some faces I want to see. But I don't and my heart breaks at the thought. Jesus comes toward me. He reaches out and wipes the tears from my face and places a crown on my head.

A golden city glimmers off in the distance.

He tells me that it is ok to put the coffee down anywhere I'd like.

"For the Lord Himself will descend from heaven with a shout, with the voice of the archangel and the trumpet of God, and the dead in Christ will rise first. Then we who are alive and remain will be caught up together with them in the clouds to meet the Lord in the air, and so we shall always be with the Lord. Comfort one another with these words."

1 Thessalonians 4:16-18

Communion

Oh Lord my God

Quiet my heart.
Allow me to ponder with mind unbridled.
Expand my imagination with the divine.
Break through my mortal dullness.
Teach me how to have communion.

Quiet my heart.
Allow me to filter out what isn't You.
Clarify my vision and my hearing.
Permit the fallen to sense the Holy.
Teach me how to have communion.

Quiet my heart.
Allow Your love to rule my day.
Refine my ragged edges.
Deliver me from my callousness.
Teach me how to have communion.

Quiet my heart.
Allow me rest in the deepest parts.
Purify my needs perceived.
Lift me above my earthy cravings.
Teach me how to have communion.

Made in the USA
San Bernardino, CA
27 October 2014